The New
African Poetry

A Three Continents Book

The New African Poetry

AN ANTHOLOGY

edited by
Tanure Ojaide
Tijan M. Sallah

LYNNE
RIENNER
PUBLISHERS

BOULDER
LONDON

Paperback edition published in the United States of America in 2000 by
Lynne Rienner Publishers, Inc.
1800 30th Street, Boulder, Colorado 80301

and in the United Kingdom by
Lynne Rienner Publishers, Inc.
3 Henrietta Street, Covent Garden, London WC2E 8LU

Published in hardcover in 1999

ISBN 0-89410-891-3 (pbk. : alk. paper)

Printed and bound in the United States of America

⊗   The paper used in this publication meets the requirements
    of the American National Standard for Permanence of
    Paper for Printed Library Materials Z39.48-1984.

    5 4 3 2 1

Contents

NORTH AFRICA

SOUTHERN AFRICA

WEST AFRICA

Acknowledgments

The editors gratefully acknowledge the poets themselves, as well as the following copyright holders, for their kind permission to reprint the poems in this anthology.

Mohammad Bennis, "Belonging to a New Family," from *Modern Arabic Poetry,* edited by Salma Khadra Jayyusi. Copyright © 1991 by Columbia University Press. Reprinted with permission of the publisher.

Abena Busia, "Exiles," "Illicit Passion," and "Mawu of the Waters," from *Testimonies of Exile,* by Abena A. Busia. Copyright © 1990 by Abena A. Busia. Reprinted with permission of Africa World Press.

Steve Chimombo, "Four Ways of Dying," from *When My Brothers Come Home: Poems from Central and Southern Africa,* edited by Frank Chipasula. Copyright © 1985 by Frank Chipasula. Published by Wesleyan University Press. Reprinted with permission of the University Press of New England.

Samuel Chimsoro, "The Curfew Breakers" and "The Change," from *Mambo Book of Zimbabwean Verse in English.* Reprinted with permission of Mambo Press.

Amal Dunqul, "The Scaffold," "Tomorrow," and "The City a Wrecked Ship," from *Modern Arabic Poetry,* edited by Salma Khadra Jayyusi. Copyright © 1991 by Columbia University Press. Reprinted with permission of the publisher.

Muhammad al-Ghuzzi, "Female," "Quatrains for Joy," and "The Pen," from *Modern Arabic Poetry,* edited by Salma Khadra Jayyusi. Copyright © 1991 by Columbia University Press. Reprinted with permission of the publisher.

Mafika Pascal Gwala, "From the Outside" and "Promise!" from *When My Brothers Come Home: Poems from Central and Southern Africa,* edited by Frank Chipasula. Copyright © 1985 by Frank Chipasula. Published by Wesleyan University Press. Reprinted with permission of the University Press of New England.

Muhammad 'Abd al-Hayy, "Ode of Signs," from *Modern Arabic Poetry,* edited by Salma Khadra Jayyusi. Copyright © 1991 by Columbia University Press. Reprinted with permission of the publisher.

Zindzi Mandela, "There's an Unknown River in Soweto" and "I Saw as a Child," from *When My Brothers Come Home: Poems from Central and Southern Africa,* edited by Frank Chipasula. Copyright © 1985 by Frank Chipasula. Published by Wesleyan University Press. Reprinted with permission of the University Press of New England.

Jack Mapanje, "Those Too Are Our Elders," "Visiting Zomba Plateau," "Making Our Clowns Martyrs," "The Cheerful Girls at Smiller's Bar, 1971," and "On Being Asked to Write a Poem for 1979," from *Chameleons and Gods,* by Jack Mapanje. Reprinted with permission of Heinemann Educational.

While every effort has been made to trace and acknowledge copyright holders, we have not been successful in all cases; in the latter situation, we decided nevertheless to publish the poems, with the intent of exposing the poets' works and advancing their reputations. We welcome any queries or corrections, so that we can amend future editions.

Introduction

Tanure Ojaide & Tijan M. Sallah

No previous anthology of poetry has attempted to bring together the African voices that started to make an impact on the world poetry scene in the mid-1970s. *The New African Poetry* assembles some of the best work of this often-called third generation and also subsequent generations of modern African poets, showing how they have gone beyond earlier generations in both form and content.

To appreciate the "new African poetry," it is important to place it in the larger historical context of the evolution of modern African poetry. We must note here that Africa has a rich oral tradition, manifested in several poetic narratives. The epics of the Mandinka king, Sunjatta, and the Zulu king, Shaka, integenerationally transmitted by *griots* or bards, are just a few examples. These classical oratures, as precursors to our literature, continue to exert strong influences on modern African poetry.

There are three distinct groups of African poets linked to distinct periods in Africa's historical evolution. The pioneering first generation of African poets, who wrote during the colonial period, includes Dennis Chukude Osadebay of Nigeria, H. I. E. Dhlomo and Benedict Wallet Vilakazi of South Africa, and Kwame Kyeretwie Boakye Danquah, Michael Dei Anang, Gladys Casely-Hayford, and R. E. G Armattoe of Ghana. These poets were not preoccupied with technique, but were concerned with themes of race, Christianity, and heroism. Much of their poetry was suffused with Biblical references, Greco-Roman allusions, and mimicry of Victorian diction. The late German Africanist, Janheinz Jahn, described these poets as engaged in an "apprentice literature" that follows European archetypes in its style and approves colonialism without argument. Dennis Osadebay's poem, "Young Africa's Thanks," is a succinct example.

> Thank you
> Sons and daughters of Britannia.
> You gave me hospitals,
> You gave me schools,
> Easy communications too,
> Your western civilization.

Lost to the uncritical voice of the typical pioneer poet were the negative aspects of colonialism, such as the wholesale obliteration of indigenous cultures, the forced labor of "natives," the siphoning of huge stocks of natural resources, the levying of unfair taxes, and the repression of local freedom.

The second generation of modern African poets came of age at the end of the colonial era, in the late 1950s and the 1960s. Critical of colonialism, their poetry was characterized by freshness of imagery, innovative use of language, and utilization of African experience to articulate a uniquely personal voice. Their poetic models were usually the best among the European practitioners: William Shakespeare, T. S. Eliot, Ezra Pound, Gerald Manley Hopkins, W. B. Yeats, and the French symbolists. From anglophone Africa, this second generation includes Gabriel Okara, Christopher Okigbo, Wole Soyinka, John Pepper Clark, Lenrie Peters, Dennis Brutus, Kofi Awoonor, Okot p'Bitek, and Kwesi Brew. From francophone Africa, there are the negritude poets such as Leopold Sedar Senghor, Tchicaya U'Tamsi, Birago Diop, and David Diop. From lusophone Africa, the best-known poets of the second generation are Agostinho Neto, Antonio Jacinto, Vasco Cabral, and Noemia de Sousa. And from Arab Africa, this generation includes Salah Abdel Sabur, Ahmad Hijazi, and Muhammad Al-Faituri.

These poets, living in a period of transition, expressed the unease at the crossroads between two cultures and the feelings of ambivalence about colonialism that ultimately translate into culture conflict. Gabriel Okara's "Piano and Drums" perhaps best symbolized this experience. Okara's poem begins: "When at break of day at a riverside / I hear jungle drums telegraphing / the mystic rhythm, urgent, raw." Later, he writes: "Then I hear a wailing piano / solo speaking of complex ways / in tear-furrowed concerto." The end of the poem dramatizes his dilemma, if not confusion: "And I, lost in the morning mist / of an age, at a riverside keep / wandering in the mystic rhythm / of jungle drums and the concerto." In Okara's poem, the drums represent African culture, while the piano represents the West. The poet does not take a position in the conflict and allows himself to be overwhelmed by the two cultures.

Kofi Awoonor's "The Weaver Bird" is a more cynical commentary on the colonial encounter: "And the weaver returned in the guise of the owner / Preaching salvations to us that owned the house." To Awoonor, religion was used to render the African submissive, thereby paving the path for his subjugation and the easy grabbing of his land by the colonialists. The feeling of anomie that followed is further depicted by Awoonor in these telling lines: "We look for new homes every day, / For new altars we strive to rebuild / The old shrines defiled by the weaver's excrement."

Yet, direct protest is not all that the poetry of the second generation exhibits. Okot p'Bitek's *Song of Lawino* is more sarcastic and borrows oral devices from his own Acoli culture to ridicule the arrogant foibles of a transient modernity: "Listen, my clansmen," the poem starts, "I cry over my husband / Whose head is lost. / Ocol has lost his head / In the forest of books." What was praised by Osadebay as something for which Africans should be thankful is excoriated by p'Bitek, as *Song of Lawino* ends: "Bile burns my inside! / I feel like vomiting! / For all our young men / Were finished in the forest, / Their manhood was finished in the class-rooms, / Their testicles / Were smashed / With large books!"

Another major theme of the second generation of modern African poets is political satire. Witnessing colonial rule, these poets felt disappointed by the African leaders who took over government from the European colonizers. They criticize the rampant corruption that followed and chronicle the political and social ills of their time. Gambian Lenrie Peters exemplifies this satiric tendency as in his "In the Beginning," in which a leader, angry at being shown the wide gap between him and his subjects, summarily orders his critic to be thrown into jail. Peters is even more interesting when he addresses personal themes such as homecoming after years of studies abroad. He writes:

> We have come home
> To the green foothills
> To drink from the cry
> Of warm and mellow birdsong.
> To the hot beaches
> Where boats go out to sea
> Threshing the ocean's harvest
> And the harassing, plunging
> Gliding gulls shower kisses on the waves.

The third generation of African poets, the subject of this anthology, includes such powerful voices as Kofi Anyidoho, Syl Cheny-Coker, Amal Dunqul, Jack Mapanje, Niyi Osundare, and Mongane Wally Serote. These poets have embraced and developed in various directions the written poetic tradition that their literary elders brought to global attention; initially, they borrowed techniques from the older poets, but they later shed these to chart and refine their own individual craft. This tendency may be seen, for example, in Senegal's Amadou Sall, whose poetry reminds us of the rich, bardic, long lines of Leopold Sedar Senghor; in Gambia's Tijan M. Sallah, whose satirical imagery recalls that of Lenrie Peters; in Ghana's Kofi Anyidoho, who reminds us of the Ewe traditional cadences of Kofi Awoonor; in Nigeria's Odia Ofeimun, who reminds us of the Yoruba/Shakespearean syncretism of Wole Soyinka; and in Egypt's Ahmed Taha, who reminds the reader of the rebellious mysticism of Amal Dunqul. Nonetheless, the new generation of African poets appears to reject the Western imitative aspects found in the poetic techniques of the earlier generations.

The sixty-two poets in this anthology are products of a period in which many witnessed civil wars, military coups, apartheid, military/civilian dictatorships, and other forms of social, economic, and political instability. They write out of experiences historically different from those of the earlier generations, which grew up in the colonial period and participated in or witnessed the nationalist struggles leading to Africa's political independence. These new poets appear to be less defensive of African cultures; they mock their cultures at times, and they tap on their people's oral traditions and techniques, which they utilize innovatively to explore the human condition in Africa.

From Senegal to Nigeria, Congo to Kenya, South Africa to Egypt, all over the continent, in place of the Pan-African sentiments that gave rise to the movements of Negritude and of African Personality, many of these new poets show more interest in their immediate societies, their separate nation-states, than in broader Pan-African issues. They see themselves as agents of change, often directing their efforts at local sociopolitical and economic issues and raging against the social ills of corruption, injustice, and economic mismanagement in their countries. They write in the hope of moving their societies toward greater social freedom.

The history of Africa from the mid-1970s has influenced these poets' preoccupation with sociopolitical and economic concerns. The coups, counter-coups, and civil wars of the late 1960s were followed by the energy crisis of the mid-1970s. Buoyant economies had then started to stagnate; and correspondingly, standards of living had started to plummet. Whereas countries like Côte d'Ivoire, Nigeria, and Zambia were relatively wealthy with a large middle class, profligate spending and economic mismanagement resulted in a generalized economic downturn with symptoms in the form of weak currencies, high unemployment, and dismal living standards. Growing corruption and the lack of democratic pluralism also exacerbated the economic problems of many of these countries. Since many of the poets in this volume witnessed firsthand the plight of the poor amid the growing self-aggrandizement of local elites in African cities, it is not surprising that many express socialist ideas, deriding the lifestyles of the political and military ruling elites and showing solidarity with workers and the masses. Angira and Cheney-Coker, among others, display in their work this concern for the underprivileged and marginalized people of their societies. Cheney-Coker, for example, speaks of the common people's agony and warns that "their patience is running out." The poets are thus generally antiestablishment and anti–status quo.

Two major characteristics of the new African poets are their self-criticism and their growing rebelliousness against tradition. They are capable of criticizing themselves, as Odia Ofeimun does in "The Poet Lied." But more important, they criticize their own nations. They do not blame all of Africa's problems on Europeans and colonialism; instead, they blame

Africans, especially African leaders, for the continent's problems. At the same time, they believe in human possibilities and are convinced of the abundant inner resources of ordinary Africans. They do not want to acquiesce to despair, despite the continent's materially low standard of living in the context of a world advancing technologically and economically into the next millennium. The conflicts in the new African poetry thus reflect not a clash of cultures between Africans and Europeans, but are mainly class-based conflicts—the exploiters vs. the exploited, the working masses vs. the indolent elite, the haves vs. the have-nots—conflicts among the "new tribes of Africa," as Kenyan writer Ngugi wa Thiongo puts it. These poets use their art to draw attention to the fundamental but often neglected aspects of their people's lives, as shown in their concern for the conservation of their natural resources and maintaining a healthy environment, as in, for example, Niyi Osundare's *The Eye of the Earth*.

There is a growing number of new poets who are rebelling against African traditional taboos, and young women are in the vanguard of this trend. The Egyptian Iman Mirsal and the Nigerian Mabel Tobrise express without inhibitions a free lifestyle that involves sex and the celebration of the female body. In "Revering Marx," Mirsal writes:

> I can't stop myself
> when I stand before a lit display window
> flourishing with underclothes,
> from thinking about Marx.

As if public seminudity is not revolutionary enough, the poet continues:

> Reverence for Marx—
> that's the single thing in common
> among those I have loved
> and allowed to pluck (at varying rates)
> some of the wild flowers on my body.

But the sarcasm is not lost at the end, where Mirsal shows how revolutionary ideas (Marxism) can be used to serve counter-revolutionary ends (sexual exploitation); how sharing ideology can be used to exploit women. The poem ends: "Marx / Marx / I will never forgive him."

Mirsal's and Tobrise's works show that women can no longer be held down by fear of patriarchal reprisals. In her simple, clear, and direct style, Mirsal, in particular, reveals aspects of women's experience—abortion, intimacy outside of marriage, and the struggle to achieve personal and intellectual identity—outside of mainstream Egyptian and Islamic values. The new female voices from all over Africa have brought novelty and a welcome dimension to the strength of the new African poetry by not only addressing women's problems but challenging the entrenched privileges of men in traditional society.

Another attribute in the new African poetry is the stylistic departure from the modernist tendencies of the second generation. No longer is form rated above content. Free verse is dominant, and the poetry aims at clarity and simplicity even when there are deeper layers of meaning. The poets want to communicate an urgent message, and their poems are crafted to serve that goal. The poetic art is seen as an avenue to sensitize the consciousness of readers in an effort to change society to be more humane and just.

Perhaps Niyi Osundare's lines best captures the credo of the new poets, if there is such a thing. Osundare says that poetry is "not the esoteric whisper / of an excluding tongue / not a claptrap / for a wondering audience / not a learned quiz / entombed in Grecoroman lore." This is obviously a reaction to the work of the second-generation poets, whose poetry was often characterized by a complex and even obscure style. The new poets look to their indigenous oral literatures for technical models for their poems. Thus, simplicity, clarity, repetition, and incantatory rhythms are common techniques.

In some of the new African poetry, there is the use of pidgin English, pidgin French, and colloquial Arabic in an attempt to loosen up and relate language and style to their concern for the underprivileged. As poems in pidgin English are popular in Nigeria and Ghana, so is "Ammiyyah poetry" in Egypt. When the parochial idiom is used, there are possibilities of humor, sarcasm, wordplay, and wit, as in Ezenwa-Ohaeto's "I wan bi President." This poem is about wanting to be an African president, in a position of luxurious tenure; free from want. It opens: "E got one dream / wey dey worry me / I don dream am tire. . . . / Di dream bi say / I wan bi President." Reminiscent of the poetic lyrics of the Nigerian musician-activist Fela Anikulapo Ramsome-Kuti, Ezenwa-Ohaeto's poem uses not only socially relevant messages but also a socially relevant language (pidgin). The poetry of the later generations is conceptualized as if it were to be read out loud, chanted, sung, or declaimed, unlike the very academic and privatist poetry associated with the second generation of African poets.

As a result of the focus on individual societies by these newer poets, one can now identify developing traits of national poetries in Africa, and also feel the unique signatures of the countries the poets represent. The South African poets, for example, write out of their recent experience of apartheid, as shown in Mafika Pascal Gwala's "From the Outside," Zindzi Mandela's "I Saw as a Child," and Mongane Wally Serote's "City Johannesburg." The Ghanaian poets, especially Kofi Anyidoho, Naana Horne, and Kojo Laing, seem to have developed a style that is peculiarly humorous and sarcastic. Common regional features can also be seen: Poets of west Africa tend to stretch the language into the realm of personal experimentation and deal with themes of political corruption and state repression; those in east and central Africa deal more with nature and are generally more temperate in their themes; the southern Africans deal with themes of racial conflict and social redemption; and the poets of northern Africa attempt to subvert Islamic orthodoxy by unveiling religious taboos.

The new African poets are also individual voices that wrestle with generational conflicts and experiences, human relationships, and existential angst. Thus, whereas social and political concerns are predominant, the poetry is difficult to pigeonhole into any reductionist categories.

We have, in our selection, attempted to cover all of geographical, political, and cultural Africa. Still, as in the cases of drama and fiction, we observe that poetry seems to flourish more in some places and in some periods of history than in others. Thus, Egypt, Ghana, Malawi, Nigeria, South Africa, Tunisia, and Zimbabwe are heavily represented in this anthology because of the current creative energy manifest there.

We have tried our utmost to include here the best and most representative of the younger African poets—men and women from all regions—to showcase the continuity, diversity, and vibrancy of recent African poetry. *The New African Poetry* clearly demonstrates that, despite the prevailing economic hardships around the continent, poetry is not only alive and well, but is a vigorous force for a revitalized continent.

CENTRAL
AND EAST AFRICA

Congo (formerly Zaire)
Kenya
Malawi
Tanzania
Uganda

Mukula Kadima–Nzuji

(b. 1947)

Born in Lumumbashi, Democratic Republic of Congo (Zaire), Kadima-Nzuji has published three collections of poems: Les Ressacs *(Kinshasa, 1969),* Prelude a la Terre *(Kinshasa, 1971), and* Redire les Mots Anciens *(Paris, 1977). The following poem was translated from the French by Gerald Moore.*

INCANTATIONS OF THE SEA:
MOANDO COAST

Shocks of dizziness
my waves, my fears of the ocean
on the salty strand of my desire.

Shocks of carnal dreams
my heaps of loosened cliff
in the bitter absence
of sap mounting to the brim of the foam.

Loosened my pollens of drunkenness
and tied and retied my seaweeds
milky way of destinies.

And I hear
stooped over the virgin insomnia
of altitudes
the savage cries of the sea
and the rough backwash of my being.

Jared Angira

(b. 1947)

Angira studied commerce at the University of Nairobi, where he edited the literature department's magazine, Busara. *He has worked in Dar es Salaam for the East African Harbours Corporation and has been Africa's representative on the International Executive Committee of the World University Service. His published poetry collections include* Juices, Silent Voices *(1972),* Soft Corals, Cascades *(1979), and* Tides of Time: Selected Poems *(1996). In many of his poems, as in* Cascades, *he sides with the poor and oppressed of his home country, Kenya.*

NEWSCAST

Listening to the newsreel today
Is like watching an open wound
A painful conscription from which you emerge
Shaking like a leaf.

Ninety lives perished
In the jumbo flame

And on the telly screen
Focused only
A small sorrow
To encourage further viewing.

One hundred killed
In a palace attack

The caster's voice, indifferent,
Marks his distant observation tower
Cinematically passing the pain
To the listener, the viewer.

As if that is not enough
Flashes the last decapitate of the mind
Late news: *Two hundred executed*
By firing squad: Imagine that, ten o'clock at night!

OBBLIGATO FROM
A PUBLIC GALLERY

The public has no belief
    In democracy:
It has mocked his expectations.

The public has no hope
    In the party;
The party partitioned his self

For the zombies are the partisans,
The public the humble listener.

The public has no confidence
    In the "nation,"
Has nationalised collectivity into individualism.

The public does not want sirens
    Of witches
have idolised them into robots.

The public has no more patience
    For philosophy
Filibustered too long with the basic needs.

The public now wants bread
At least to breed tomorrow.

The public now wants rice
At least to rise tomorrow.

The public is tired
Of following the rainbow.

The public wants to believe
That tomorrow will not be dead.

The public wants to believe
That behind tomorrow there is hope,
The conquest of man's destiny.

At least, the public wishes to sleep
In the understanding that on the morrow

He'll rise above the grave
Having conquered the long arms of contradictions.

OLD WHARF CANTO

In moments of anguish
I have even built hopes
On the glowing moon

Only, the glimmer sinks down the troubled ocean.

In moments of despair
I have incubated my eggs
In the warmth of the after–rain evaporation

Only, the warmth oozes down the troubled waters.

In moments of hope
I have visited the abandoned ship
Daring the cold solitude of the old wharves

Only, courage falls deep down the troubled waters.

What moments, shall
Idiotic diver, submerge the whirlpools
To hold up the winds for my sail?

And the troubled waters
Consume the whirlpools.

DIALOGUE

She asked me why I did such things:
I looked at the Sun, it shone at will.
She asked me when I'll do all that I should have done:
I thought of the rains that fall at will.
She asked me why I failed to fulfill my words:
The balance of payments rocked in a whirling mess.
She asked me why like the dumb I sat:
I thought of the stub of words, the blood they leave.
She asked me why I never laughed:
I thought of men who laugh in tears.
She asked me why no tango I danced:
And I recalled the cripples who'd never stood upright.
She asked me why I'd suddenly stopped to sprint like the hart:
I looked down the west and saw the sun sink slowly down.
She asked me why I was happy no more:
Across the sky I saw the rainbow arc
Across the road a mirage shone and quickly fled
And I recalled the dreams of the previous night.
She demanded the best the world could give.
And I recalled the rabble who had no vote.
She asked me why my life had rolled down the slopes
And I recalled the many tombs in the deserted vale.

SYMPHONY FROM THE BALCONY

Sometimes I sit in the balcony
   And watch the rivers of the world
Flow down the many deltas
   Impatiently awaited by the ocean deeps

Sometimes I watch
   The young birds of the air
Leave their parents to make a living
   But all in a pair, face to the world

When I long for peace
   Mind hovers with the quails
Knowing too well
   However tired the wings no landing on tree

When therefore I gather my selves
   Scattered like the rivers on land
I long for their waters
   To lead to the sea

And we all wish
   That after these travels
All scattered feelings
   Would converge
On that ocean, the livid.

Steve Chimombo

(b. 1945)

Born in Zomba, Chimombo was educated at Chancellor College, University of Malawi; the University of Wales; the University of Leeds; and Columbia University, where he received an Ed.D. He has been teaching for many years at Chancellor College. The director of Writers and Artists Services International, he also edits WASI, *a magazine for the arts. He has published a collection of poems titled* Napolo and the Python *(1994); a novel,* The Basket Girl *(1990); a collection of short stories,* Tell Me a Story *(1992); and two plays,* The Rainmaker *(1978) and* Wachiona Ndani? *(1992). His scholarly works include* Malawian Oral Literature *(1988). His poems rely heavily on the indigenous myths of his people.*

OF PROMISES AND PROPHECY

Prologue

Tomorrows reactivate somnolence
todays perpetuate inertia
yesterdays diffuse dismembered hopes:
the eternal miasma of zombies,

smeared in disco lights
lacerated with reggae sounds
groping in the darkness between
the tavern, bar, and rest house:

progress punctuated by puddles
of vomit, sweat, beer, and wine,
the whore's smile and the thug's
demand for a light or else.

I

No, they shall not have the truth
for facts are explosives
in anonymous brown bags
exploding between the fingers,
blowing reality into oblivion.

Let the few remaining honest souls
still roaming dangerously abroad
be lured again into the folds
of festering falsehood.
Let common knowledge become
the property of the minority
and mystification be manna
and hyssop for the masses.

And so, after taking some
for one or two rides
let us recede into the citadels
of silence and feed the people
with more lines of lies.

And under the shroud of silence
let retrospection unroll the map,
trace the tracks of introspection
to pinpoint where the derailment
and mass burial of truth took place.

II

No, don't jog memory anymore,
let it coil as harmless
as a puffadder until it's stepped upon,
only add more fuel to the amnesia,
programmed inertia and somnolence.

Let the few tumescent egos still around
mass–produce psychic onanism,
pack them into portable and compact
shapes that will fit into trunks, cases,
bags, pocket books, and passports
saleable at the next port of entry.

Educate the masses with new tools
of ideological bio–feedback
irrigate their drought–stricken spirits with
technological fried–while–you–starve
computerized mind–swooping, malaise,
anomy, and emotional dehydration.

Arm the beggars, vagrants, peasants
with transistorized pleas, canned laughter,
mesmerize the workers with videotaped leisure,
press–gang local witches into astronauts,
cauterize hope, desire, and memory.

Where are the great plans now?
Where the blueprints?
What is the programme?
What now?

Epilogue

Shall I destroy the citadel
and rebuild it in three days?
Three days in which will rise
a monolith of groans, gasps, and gashes
that are mouths screaming silent,
soul–searing, razor–sharp agony?

Three days in which will sprout
a luxurious green gold garden
with patches of marinas, mazdas,
fiats, fords, buicks, and benzes?

Armed with a multi-pronged plan
Man-Against-Self-and-Society (MASS)
I descended from the mountain top
with a blueprint of self-raising ideology,
improved-me conditions,
modern methods of mass-hypnosis,
and broke the citadels of silence.

FOUR WAYS OF DYING

The celebrants chanted
to the reluctant martyrs-to-be:
We would have a blood sacrifice!

The Crab's response:
I crawl
in my shell sideways,
                    backwards,
                    forwards;
Avoid

            direct action on public matters,
            confrontation,
            commitment;
Meander

            to confuse direction or purpose,
                                    meaning,
                                    sense;
Squat

            to balance the issues
            weigh,
            consider.

The Chameleon's answer:
Until I have exhausted my wardrobe,
lost my dye to a transparent nothingness,
free of reflection, true to my image,
I'll match my colours with yours,
snake my tongue out to your fears,
bare my teeth to puncture your hopes,
tread warily past your nightmares,
curl my tail round your sanctuaries,
clasp my pincer legs on your veins,
to listen to your heart beat.

The Mole's descent:
Wormlike I build in the entrails of the earth,
fashion intricate passages and halls,
tunnel Utopias and underground Edens,
substitute surface with subterranean vision,
level upon level of meaning of existence,
as I sink downwards in my labyrinth,
to die in a catacomb of my own making.

The *Kalilombe*'s ascent:
The gestation and questioning are over,
I'm restless with impatient foetuses,
belly-full with a profusion of conundrums.
My pilgrimage takes me to the cradle,
the *nsolo* tree, the lie-in of man's hopes.
I grit my teeth, grab the slippery surface
and hoist myself up the nation's trunk.
On the topmost branch I have momentary
possession of eternity whirling in the chaosis,
with the deathsong floating from my lips,
I fling myself down on Kaphirintiwa rock
as multivarious forms of art and life
issue out from the convulsions
of the ruptured womb;
and thus I die.

Frank Chipasula

(b. 1949)

Born in Malawi, Chipasula studied at both Chancellor College, Zomba, and the University of Zambia. He received an M.A. in creative writing and a Ph.D. in English from Brown University. A founding member of the Writers Group at Chancellor College, he has published two collections of poetry, titled Visions and Reflections *and* Whispers on Wings *(1991). He edited* When My Brothers Come Home: Poems from Central and Southern Africa *(1985), and with his wife, Stella,* The Heinemann Book of African Women's Poetry *(1995). Chipasula currently teaches at the University of Nebraska, Omaha. His poetry deals primarily with his exile from the dictatorship of Kamuzu Banda.*

MANIFESTO ON ARS POETICA

My poetry is exacting a confession
from me: I will not keep the truth from my song.
I will not bar the voice undressed by the bees
from entering the gourd of my bow–harp.
I will not wash the blood off the image;
I will let it flow from the gullet
Slit by the assassin's dagger through
The run–on line until it rages in the verbs of terror;
And I will distil life into the horrible adjectives.
I will not clean the poem to impress the tyrant;
I will not bend my verses into the bow of a praise song.

I will put the symbols of murder hidden in high offices
In the centre of my crude lines of accusations.
I will undress our land and expose her wounds.
I will pierce the silence around our land with sharp metaphors,
And I will point the light of my poems into the dark
Nooks where our people are pounded to pulp.
I will not coat my words in lumps of sugar
But serve them to our people with the bitter quinine.
I will not keep the truth from my heartstringed guitar;
I will thread the voice from the broken lips
Through my volatile verbs that burn the lies.
I will ask only that the poem watch the world closely;
I will ask only that the image put a lamp on the dark
Ceiling in the dark sky of my land and light the dirt.
Today, my poetry has exacted a confession from me.

A LOVE POEM FOR MY COUNTRY

For James

I have nothing to give to you, but my anger
And the filaments of my hatred reach across the border.
You, you have sold many and me to exile.
Now shorn of precious minds, you rely on
What hands can grow to build your crumbling image.

Your streets are littered with handcuffed men
And the drums are thuds of the warden's spiked boots.
You wriggle with agony as the terrible twins, law and order,
Call out the tune through the thick tunnels of barbed wire.

Here, week after week, the walls dissolve and are slim,
The mist is clearing and we see you naked like
A body that is straining to find itself but cannot
And our hearts are thumping with pulses of desire or fear
And our dreams are charred chapters of your history.

My country, remember I neither blinked nor went to sleep;
My country, I never let your life slide downhill
And passively watched you, like a recklessly driven car,
Hurrying to your crash, while the driver leapt out.

The days have lost their song and salt;
We feel bored without our free laughter and voice
Every day thinking the same and discarding our hopes.
Your days are loud with clanking cuffs
On men's arms as they are led away to decay.

I know a day will come and wash away my pain
And I will emerge from the night breaking into song
Like the sun, blowing out these evil stars.

THE SINGING DRUM

For Nabanda
from a Nyanja folktale

Your sweet voice is trapped in the drum
That sings praises to a gelded lion
Whose magic tail lured you back to the river
Where his wide-mouthed drum awaited your voice.
He put out his claws, caressed you lovingly
As you searched for your lost waist beads,
And tamed you into his hoarse drum.
Now he bleeds you for his coffers amid drunken
Orgies: between your fat haunches flow coerced
Gifts: fourteen thousand eggs, a century of goats,
You dance out innumerable chickens, granaries
Of maize, flocks of sheep ooze out as you wail
Sweetly from feast to feast to feats of false
Heroics and histrionics in a hail of slogans.
You sing out a million Kwacha at a time
Into the Swiss banks, as your accordion-ribbed
babies shrivel and shrink at your ample nipples.
Sister, your sweet voice wails in a foreign drum.

EVERYTHING TO DECLARE

Zonse
Zonse zimene za . . .

The Special Branch are after my neck.
I tell them my neck is too thin—
Never mind, they say, we love the slim ones too.
I tell them my shadow is too narrow
They want that too, they covet it:
That too is dangerous, they insist.

Take my shadow and its umbrella trees
My tears and my eyes and all my bright suns—
I declare no possession that you detest:
Look through my intestines and hear what drums there
Gentlemen, do not forget anything of these treasures:
Strip me of my dark skin, my free thoughts, lop off
These arms like the Portuguese *toropas*
Amputated Frelimo genitals, arms, and legs.

Bring in your python lanterns and their viper eyes
Let your hound dogs sniff in every nook—
Take everything therein except my personal shadow.
Take the sunsets and clawing nights, save my dream.
You would not allow me one little breath
Or one last glance at those bright copper sands.
Today, I ask you to destroy me, but my phantom:
That is the right spelling of your own destruction.
Take the ornaments also and their joyous sparkle—
But leave the mortar—I will start the world afresh.

DOUBLE SONG

For Seamus Heaney

Enter the forest
carefully:
A little birdsong
threatens
to burst out
of your heart
caged as a bird
and
flow like a deep
river.

Leave the forest
stealthily:
A little river
struggles
to break out
of the barbed trees
whose roots drink blood
and
flow like a bulbous
song.

Did you notice
the dove's eggs
in the barbed wire nest?
Your words are very close
to what is happening.

Jack Mapanje

(b. 1945)

Born of Yao and Nyanja parents in Kadango Village, southern Malawi, Mapanje studied at Chancellor College, Zomba, and the University of London, where he received a Ph.D. in linguistics. He taught for many years at Chancellor College, where he founded and directed the Writers Group and edited Kalulu, *a journal of oral literature. He has published two collections of poetry, titled* Of Chameleons and Gods *(1981) and* The Birds of Mikuyu Prison *(1993). He was detained without charge from September 1987 until his release in May 1991 for the publication* Of Chameleons and Gods. *His detention generated considerable protest from human rights and writers' organizations worldwide and he was given an award, received by Wole Soyinka on his behalf, at the 1988 Poetry International in Rotterdam. Since his release from prison, he has been living in York, UK. One of the leading new African poets, his poetry is suffused with the oral literature of his people. In addition to being disciplined in form, his poetry carries subtle satire, dry humor, and sarcasm.*

THESE TOO ARE OUR ELDERS

Watch these elders. They always come at night
In bloated plumage, tossing you on their
Avocado noses, inhaling all the free air out
Of you. Their masks carry fatal viruses.

One came the other night draped in hyena skins
His face showing amid the fluffed–out ostrich
Feathers, twisting his sinews in a frenzied
Dance. At work I was unseating him, he preached.

But I too went to the village he had visited.
They said I should ask him next time why
He always came at night, why he pretended
I was more useful than the Whiteman once in

My seat, and why he sent me to school at all?
Well, he merely backslid through the bamboo rafters
Showering behind rotten amulets and mice shit!
Why do these elders always exploit our disbelief?

VISITING ZOMBA PLATEAU

Could I have come back to you to wince
Under the blur of your negatives,
To sit before braziers without the glow
Of charcoal, to cringe at your rivers
That without their hippos and crocs
Merely trickle gratingly down, to watch
Dragonflies that no longer fascinate and
Puff-adders that have lost their puff?
Where is your charming hyena tail—
Praying-mantis who cared for prayers once?
Where is the spirit that touched the hearts
Lightly—chameleon colours of home?
Where is your creation myth? Have I come
To witness the carving and jingling only of
Your bloated images and piddling mirrors?

MAKING OUR CLOWNS MARTYRS
(OR RETURNING HOME
WITHOUT CHAUFFEURS)

We all know why you have come back home with no
National colours flanking your black mercedes benz.
The radio said the toilets in the banquet halls of
Your dream have grown green creepers and cockroaches
Which won't flush, and the orders you once shouted
To the concubines so mute have now locked you in.
Hard luck my friend. But we all know what currents
Have stroked your temper. You come from a breed of
Toxic frogs croaking beside the smoking marshes of
River Shire, and the first words you breathed were
Snapped by the lethal mosquitoes of this morass.
We knew you would wade your way through the arena
Though we wondered how you had got chosen for the benz.
You should have been born up the hills, brother where
Lake waters swirl and tempers deepen with each season
Of the rains. There you'd see how the leopards of
Dedza hills comb the land or hedge before their assault.
But welcome back to the broken reed–fences, brother;
Welcome home to the poached reed–huts you left behind;
Welcome to these stunted pit–latrines where only
The pungent whiff of buzzing green flies gives way.
You will find your idle ducks still shuffle and fart
In large amounts. The black dog you left still sniffs
Distant recognition, lying, licking its leg–wounds. And
Should the relatives greet you with nervous curiosity
In the manner of masks carved in somebody's image,
There is always across the dusty road, your mad auntie.
She alone still thinks this new world is going shit.
She alone still cracks about why where whys are crimes.

THE CHEERFUL GIRLS
AT SMILLER'S BAR, 1971

The prostitutes at Smiller's Bar beside the dusty road
Were only girls once in tremulous mini-skirts and oriental
Beads, cheerfully swigging Carlsbergs and bouncing to
Rusty simanje-manje and rumba booming in the juke-box.
They were striking virgins bored by our Presbyterian
Prudes until a true Presbyterian came one night. And like
To us all the girls offered him a seat on cheap planks
In the dark backyard room choked with diesel-oil clouds
From a tin-can lamp. Touched the official rolled his eyes
To one in style. She said no. Most girls only wanted
A husband to hook or the fruits of Independence to taste
But since then mini-skirts were banned and the girls
Of Smiller's Bar became "ugly prostitutes to boot!"

Today the girls still giggle about what came through
The megaphones: the preservation of our traditional
et cetera . . .

ON BEING ASKED
TO WRITE A POEM FOR 1979

Without kings and warriors occasional verse fails

Skeletal Kampuchea children staring, cold
Stubborn Irish children throwing grenades
These are objects too serious for verse,
Crushed Soweto children clutching their entrails
Then in verse bruised, mocks

Today no poet sufficiently asks why dying children
Stare or throw bombs. And why should we
Compute painful doubts that will forever occupy us?
Talking oil-crises in our eight-cylinder cars
Is enough travesty . . .

The year of the child must make no difference then
Where tadpoles are never allowed to grow into frogs!

Lupenga Mphande

(b. 1947)

Born in Thoza, northern Malawi, Mphande attended the University of Malawi, Lancaster (England), and the University of Texas, Austin, where he received a Ph.D. A founding member of the Malawi Writers Workshop, he was a literary critic for the Malawi Broadcasting Corporation and the editor of Odi, *a bilingual Malawian journal of literature. He taught at the University of Malawi before leaving for the United States, where he has been teaching at Ohio State University. His poetry draws its strength from childhood experiences and the environment.*

I WAS SENT FOR

I was sent for,
As happens in the country. That morning,
I lit the mine shaft for the last time
And proceeded in haste on the long journey home:
Miles by air, miles by land, Welkom to Mzimba.
I travelled through gentle land peopled with white thorns,
On a day that looked endless.
As I approached my village kraal in rainless heat
A pair of wagtails rose to a roof, whistling in flight,
Bobbing and darting; in the sadness of their whistles
I heard my wife's voice telling of "reprisals"
Mounted against our people, our charred countryside
Our hungry children. She had written,
"The government thinks we are the enemy!"
I remembered our ancestors in rock paintings,
Forever trapped in the searing granite.
I looked at the trees and thought, "A curse on informers!
For our children's sake we must fight."
I have been sent for. It has happened before in our country.

WALKING THE PLATEAU

I can't look at all at these lush fields of Hoho
Without thinking of Kaliyangile, the hermit
Who cultivated millet, pumpkin, and musaka
To chase away kwashiorkor from his village.
I can't look at the rolling plateaux beyond
Without thinking of Chimbekeya, who blacksmithed
Old guns, and taught me how to hunt,
Moulded gunpowder from goat dung,
And in the season hunted with the bee.
Fed with the otter, I cannot at all walk through
the Vipya and watch hippopotami cross placid lagoons,
Slithering, appearing and disappearing in gambols,
Or cranes, flamingoes, pelicans, herons, kingfishers scuddling
Along river banks, and flocks of small birds, brilliant and swift
Flash from reeds, rise out of sight—I can't watch all this
Without thinking of the Dwambazi of my childhood.

PAIN

I have the itch on my nape
all herbs in the bush have failed to cure
I can't even wear my suit now
And every time I don a neck-tie it's
itch . . . itch . . . itch . . .

My sister has a wart on her dimple
All modern cosmetics have failed to trim
She can't even spruce up herself now
And every time she wears make-up it's
dimple . . . dimple . . . dimple . . .

My father has the grips in his groin
All medicinemen's charms have failed to heal
He can't even till the land now
And every time he rises to hoe it's
creak . . . creak . . . creak . . .

My mother has a tingle in her nipple
All her baby-nestling has failed to tame
She can't even perform the matanje dance anymore,
And every time she carries a baby now
A chill nips her back and burns like fire.

Edison Mpina

(b. 1950?)

Mpina works in a bank in Blantyre, Malawi. He is featured in Summer Fires: New Poetry of Africa, *edited by Angus Calder, Jack Mapanje, and Cosmo Pieterse (1983).*

REBORN

Now I am like a seaweed
That's been washed to land
I've cashed my last drop of salt

Walking from Mount Soche Hotel
Down to the Blantyre City Hall
My eyes, like the skin beyond the blister wall
And my steps with a hangover of last year
Still tell about me
Like darkness in moonlight

Before this civilization
I lived both hands on my lifewheel;
I slept in trees, falling like a tipsy monkey
I strolled in graveyards like a witch
To avoid police paths

Prison was nevertheless my homestead
Its uniform crackling like a dry mango leaf
Was the only clothing I couldn't evade
Its monthly stew, like stale bread in a child's pants,
Was the most palatable food I ate
And the hairless mountain peak
Peering over the mossy prison walls
Was the only sightseeing I did

Now, abroad without belts of chains
and breathing newly born air
With female lovers
And touching shoulders with patrol policemen
You can all watch the free match
On the saltless field where I'm reborn.

SUMMER FIRES OF MULANJE MOUNTAIN

Your matronly face is
blood-red like the flesh of a water-melon;
Smoke is rising ascension-like
through your hair . . . you have
become a burning field of neon

Skin to skin bonfires to
awaken mountain shrines? No, for
these are fires lit by angry heat . . .
Power generated by summer

Unfailing reminder of
age-long lomwe* tribal icons,
the fires paint veins of dried rivers
and sculpt faces of dead relatives
as they burn every summer.

---

lomwe: communal name of people who live around Mount Mulanje.

Freddy Macha

Macha is a journalist in Dar es Salaam, Tanzania.

AN ARTIST AND A WAILING MOTHER

While I sit down scribbling herring verses
walking along streets of written songs
dancing in the terraces of evening recitals
chiming guitars and drums to voices of poems and music

a plaintive question raises a hand
an ailing gesture of a wailing mother

"What shall I eat, my son?" she asks
She talks of money to buy khangas*
she talks of money to buy rice and beans and shoes
and money to take a sick brother to hospital

While I walk about in swimming-pools of flute music
my hand laboured to scribble whistling songs
my neck choked with a tie of evening recitals and music
a plaintive query watches me with a tear
a wailing gesture of a wailing woman

"What shall I eat my son?"
She can't cry—she can't laugh
she watches my poetry
and she is still hungry
seeing nothing in it
and I continue to write verses
haunted by her poor voice

---

*khangas: lengths of colorful cloth worn by east African women.

CORRUPTION

A young clerk peruses the court's files.
Somewhere along the table, a fly zzzzz past with the car's horn
blaring outside

The young clerk is tense;
that image of a pregnant wife
lying
painfully
hungrily
at the Ocean Road Hospital bed
whispers something in his heart's ears

"Destroy the file for me" zooms the rapacious voice
of the big-bellied man who just left him a while ago;
the appeal limps in his veins
waving a flag of those red-pinkish 1,000 shillings notes

no more pains
no more taxi-worries
the mother shall carry the new-born baby home
comfortably

Suddenly the court's file is in shreds.
Its white smiling pieces laugh loudly
applauding
the wish
of the rich bureaucrat
that has just been
implemented

Assumpta Acam–Oturu

(b. 1953)

Born in Teso, eastern Uganda, Acam-Oturu received a diploma in journalism from Mindolo Ecumenical Centre in Zambia. She later received a B.A. in journalism and international relations from the University of California in 1983. She currently works for a radio station in Los Angeles.

AN AGONY . . . A RESURRECTION

The seven hills shudder in silence,
Agony, pain and anguish
As the heavy guns thunder
And incessantly rock these hills
Interrupting nothing, nothing

For it was a familiar sound
A living reality of this land
A sound that had redirected this country's course;
Once prosperous, once the pearl of Africa,
Once the pride of its people,
Now sundered by hatred, soured by grief,
Now longing for revenge on itself.

For twenty years, blood has written
This country's history
Yet from the gentle heart come the waters
Flowing in patience, pride
As forever transforms the deserts afar—
A water—the Nile that swallowed
The corpses time couldn't bury.

On the seven hills stood beauty
From it one could see what one wanted to see
Ignore what one didn't want to see
But it was there, right before one's eyes:
Anarchy, conflict, confusion, corruption, ideology,
Slogan, that only feed this land with corpses
The skulls of Luwero, the monuments of Luwero
Now only tell, and inscribe in blood.

Rich in patience and hope, this land has waited
Under the perennial sun in those twenty years
The dawns of those years were a prayer, a rise in hope.
As her ravaged arteries bled to waste
A voice from the stream could only yell: never, never again!
Was it too early, or was the voice
Now drowning into the gory sunset
A transition that may one day draw
From its unknown source, a resurrection, a new spirit?

NORTH AFRICA

Egypt
Morocco
Sudan
Tunisia

Abdul Maqsoud
Abdul Karim

(b. 1956)

Born in Mansurah, Abdul Karim holds both a B.Sc. and an M.Sc. in neuro-psychiatry from Ain Shams University and is currently working on a doctorate in psychiatry. One of the "Aswat" (antiestablishment) young Egyptian poets, Abdul Karim belongs to the Seventies' poets who first began publishing after the wars with Israel and the subsequent peace accord. His three poetry publications include The Dream Descends with the Dreamer *(1993). The two poems here are taken from* Azdahim bilma-malik 88 *(1992). He has also translated four books from English to Arabic. He uses pre-Islamic imagery to express his private experiences rather than to express Arab values and identity. The two poems below were translated from the Arabic by Clarissa C. Burt.*

NIGHTMARE I

The tribe forsook you
or the beloved forsook you—what's the difference?
Abdu, you'll rest in death
the grave will eat your corpse.
What's the difference if the beloved eats you,
or if snakes eat you?
Abdu, don't be so sad.
The tribe forsook you, and the slandering homeland;
the ass tripped you up. You fell,
you spilled the ewe's milk
and you stepped on the tail of your mother's cat.
You slept, and the angel gave you dust juice to drink;
you rode devils.

Abdu you've spilled the milk.
I scream. Mother your teat has dried up!
I scream. You knead cemetery cakes from my blood
on the fortieth day of mourning.
You, Abdu, are an accursed slave;
and you, forsaken one—you've spilled the tribe's milk.
Your father weeps in his grave, your mother weeps at home.
You are obstinate, you lift the question up,
    you put the question down

    What's the difference?

NIGHTMARE III

I am storing at heart a bundle of grass
and a jar of water
I erect a tent for me from your crumbs
I invite ewes to graze my valley
I let out a beautiful dog to protect them
from the wailing of my blood.
The heart is wide enough for all the tribe's ewes.

The ewes reject my heart
the rams butt my heart
my beautiful dog bites my blood,
he slaps my right cheek and my left cheek
he slaps my sorrow.
I open my heart's coffer
out of it come ruined encampments
   collapsing cities
   bodies of children
   bodies of women
   bodies of men
I lose them on the way from grace to Afterlife
Hellfire is promised me
I open my heart's coffer
I lose its children.

Amal Dunqul

(1940-1982)

Dunqul was born in Upper Egypt (Nile Valley). Though he did not complete his formal education, his first collection of poetry, Maqtal al-Qamar (The Murder of the Moon), *published in 1974, earned the respect of critics for its vitality. He was a controversial actor during the rule of Anwar Sadat because he opposed the improved ties with Israel at the expense of other Arab countries. During his short life, he published six collections of poetry, the best known of which is* The Coming Testament *(1975). Dunqul has been called the "last of the jahiliyya poets"[1] (the pre-Islamic poets), and younger Egyptian poets, like Ahmed Taha and the Eighties' poets, revere him. The three poems were translated from the Arabic by Sharif Elmusa and Thomas G. Ezzy.*

THE SCAFFOLD

You shout and hurry through
the rows of soldiers.
We kiss. At last, the moment:
at the last step
of the scaffold's ladder
I feel your face.
You are beyond me now.
Are you my child
or my widowed mother?
I feel your face . . .

(I am blind.
They have bound my eyes
and hands with the folder
of my confessions.
The authorities will go through it,
authenticate my statements and my
signature . . .
Perhaps it was the interrogator
who added the sentence
that sends me to my death.
And yet they promised they would give me back
my eyes and hands
after a fair trial . . .)

The era of death is not yet over,
my grieving child.
I am not the first one to predict
the age of earthquakes,
nor am I the first
to have said out in the marketplace
that in its nest the dove is perched upon a bomb.

I will pass my secrets to your lips.
I will pass my only desire on
to you, to the sheaf of wheat,
to next year's flower.

Kiss me, and do not cry.
Do not let the cloud of fear
block me from your eyes
in this heavy moment.
Already between us there are
too many iron mantles.
Do not add a new one . . .

TOMORROW

When you get there, do not greet them.
Now they are carving up your children
on their platters;
they have charred your nest,
set fire to the straw
and sheaves of wheat . . .
Tomorrow it is you they will slay
and dig for treasures
in your craw
Tomorrow, our ancient cities
will turn into cities of tents
pitched along a stairway
to the scaffold.

THE CITY A WRECKED SHIP

I feel I am alone tonight;
and the city, with its ghosts and tall
buildings, is a wrecked ship
that pirates looted long ago
and sent to the ocean's bottom.
At that time the captain leaned his head
against the railing. Beneath his feet
lay a broken wine bottle, shards
of a precious metal. And the sailors
clung to the silent masts,
and through their ragged clothes
swam sad fish of memory.
Silent daggers, growing moss, baskets
of dead cats . . . Nothing pulses
in this acquiescent world.

Iman Mirsal

(b. 1966)

Born in Mansurah, Mirsal holds a B.A. in Arabic literature from Mansurah University and an M.A. in modern Arabic literature from Cairo University. Mirsal belongs to a group of poets known as the Nineties' poets, and may be one of its most promising voices. She has published three collections of poetry, including A Dim Passage to Learn Dancing *(1995) and* Walking as Long as Possible *(1997). Her poetry, according to Clarissa C. Burt, is "simple, direct and clear; her work reveals aspects of women's experience outside of mainstream values, discussing experiences of abortion, intimacy outside of marriage, and the struggle to achieve personal and intellectual identity with quick-cutting incisiveness."[2] Her poetry is lyrical and rebels against traditional Arabic poetry. The three poems below were translated from the Arabic by Clarissa Burt.*

ABORTION

Since that day
irrespective of the empty packaging
and the carefully stuffed plastic bags
and the number of garbage men out to clean up Cairo
I say to myself
No doubt inside these caravans brimming with
    household leavings
there are
still
in the cotton which is no longer white
lots of foetuses
    with eyes wider than horror
    unable to point out the wombs which miscarried them.

CONFESSIONS

No doubt I need a year of hallucinating
for I must say to my father
that the one man who broke me off of desiring him
resembled him completely.
I must tell my friends: I have perfect pictures of my face
all of them are true, all of them are me
I'll distribute them to you one by one.
I have to say to my lover: Thank my blessed infidelities . . .
Were it not for them, I would not have waited all this time
to discover an exceptional void in your laugh.
As for me, I'm about set to make a scandal of myself
to hide behind.

I USUALLY LOOK AROUND ME

With the awareness of a creature awaiting some kind of collapse
I usually look around me
perhaps because of this
my neck has a strength inconsonant with my body
The surprising thing
is that I don't expect a live bullet
from empty side streets
nor even tank tracks
as a local means of killing,
but the utterly passing collision
of eyes—which I almost know—
yet are able to do the deed.

Ahmed Taha

(b. 1948)

Born in Cairo, Taha is a major new voice in Egyptian poetry. One of the Seventies' poets, he uses pre-Islamic imagery for private experiences. He identifies, as Clarissa C. Burt observes, with "the sa'aluk, the vagabond poet who has dissociated himself from tribal affiliation, and scorned the system of tribal social structure and values."³ In addition to the five poems below, Clarissa Burt also translated from the Arabic two of his recent collections, titled Empire of Surrounding Walls *and* Table 48.

ABODE OF ARRIVAL

Like a minaret
or tomb I rose before you
garbed in palmtrees . . .
So how did you lay bare my guises—you roused
this long recumbency, you named me
with letters and applied attributes to me.
Places became too confined for me . . .
    I made words my profession
I bespoke the stones of my race, and its trees
       endowed with speech; I made love to its rivers
          and the dirt of the fields . . .
The herbage bespoke me in the wasteland . . .
Now I have a race
of words, a throne the breadth of heaven
and earth
I fenced it in with ribs, readied
my horses and said: I am leaving my race
to alight in a land without speech . . .
Don't let my heart bolt on me!

Shall I repeat what I said yesterday
or debate this obliteration of self
and run
as if I were a demigod?

STATE OF BUTTERFLY

Thus . . .
He now begins his wakefulness
     like the bats
     and gods
He brings forth the sun from the pocket
     of his housepants, and lets out
     an exaltation for the morning
       and there awaken
     Words, and run to him
     a congregation:
         of bread
         tobacco
         and naked women

Yet . . .
Perhaps there comes—isolately—a face
from the companions of the past . . .
Asking him:
     How did the first days come to an end
     more quickly than God had set down?
Sometimes
     he stabs a letter or two
     and the face dissolves
     and the names mix up
Sometimes
     the dawn call to prayer goes off
     darkness pervades
     and he sleeps

Sometimes
    he would postpone the sun's dispatch
    for a day or two—
    the room is too confined
        for the putrid naked bodies
        and tobacco smoke
        and the corpses of words.

ARABESQUE

There's a screen of arabesque between us and them
which cannons lick and prayer rites uphold,
through its perforations generals and casualties exchange
    skulls
        crescents
            native lands
                and military decorations.
On its two sides there crowd about
    maniacs
        lepers
            the blind
                and rag–clad mystics.
Every body which passes into it
goes right through,
every heart which traverses it
burns up.

DECEMBER 31

Thus
Egyptians roam about, as roam hippo-
potami
next to their graves
forgetting lands beyond the river,
drawing close together
and closer.
Not they, horses taking off into the heart

of the desert;
not they, fishes opening a sluicegate to the sea
and sluicegates to forgetfulness.
So why, away from home, do you carry a saddlebag
of ruined encampments?
You vagabond in the world alone
searching for a street resembling Shubra
and a cafe resembling the Bustan
You enter a bar you call the Warehouse
conversing with bodies of terra cotta
and faces resembling tombs
topped with wax,
color–coated.
There you are, speaking to them in prose,
losing your primary characteristics.
The brown leg asks you,
so you extend your eye afar
and point to Opera Bar
and stretch out your legs and touch the base
of the statue.
You drink two glasses with broad bean sprouts
crunching the sparrow carcass with dogteeth.
You hear the chirping
and think how the world's sparrows
had landed in Opera's bars;
knowing this abundant etiquette they came
obediently between your canine teeth.
Did the hoopoe bird lead them astray, that former
General in the Army of Solomon?
Or were they sauteed in oil by a civilian president?
You have to have your tenth glass
or leave the bar counter
and enter the circle of the endangered . . .

WALL OF DREAMS (2)

But I
am not an isolated god
searching for an empty heaven,
nor am I deprived of cafes
and bars.
I sit on the doorstep of my house
not incapable of love;
I write poetries on women . . .
Only
I need a political party to pull together my members
and give me one number
I can memorize
or a dictator
who doffs his helmet when he sees me,
who shoves bullets into my heart
just as grandparents shove candy
into the palms of children.

Mohammad Bennis

(b. 1948)

Born and educated in Morocco, Bennis has been the editor of *Al-Thaqafa
Al-Jadida* (New Culture). *In addition to a critical study of contemporary
Moroccan poetry, he has published four collections of poetry, including*
Before Speech *(1969),* Something About Joy and Oppression *(1972), and* A
Face Shining Across the Stretch of Time *(1974). The poem below was
translated from the Arabic by Sharif Elmusa and Charles Doria.*

BELONGING TO A NEW FAMILY

My father recommended safety
fearing to contradict law and order
he memorized the legal code, advised me:
if you're wise, stay out of politics

But how crowded courts and prisons have become
how gallows have swung, bullets whined
how much blood shed, enveloped castles of anger and mutiny
down through the ages!

How this question turns colorless, emptied of meaning
                whether I dream or wake?
How the silence that reigns behind numb curtains
slips away in the absence, pierces walls
and becomes tablets of wrath? How such curtains reveal
voices spreading on flame to bring us to the massacres of history?

How can we sit on chairs, strapped down by advice
recommending safe submission?
How return?
        Without taking action
        words lie dead on library shelves
        canned in manuscripts, newspapers, books

Rachida Madani

(b. 1953)

Born and currently living in Tangier, Madani published a collection of poems titled Femme Je Suis *(1981). The poem below was translated from the French by Eric Sellin.*

HERE I AM ONCE MORE . . .

Here I am once more before the sea
smashing whole doors against the rocks
mingling in the same bitter rolling motion
sand and pearls
in the burning metallic waves
the jasmine of my childhood and the shriek–owl of hell.

Here I am once more before the sea, bent over
under the annual booty of rancour
of fatigue
and of cocks slaughtered throats cut to no avail
for the well–being of a turban
which for a long time now has been
no more than a heap of dust
smirking under a slab
while in the shade of a fig tree
women and candles burn
to do magic with the eye
bad luck
and the raven of despair.

For an amulet did I too
swap my gold tooth
and the henna on my hands
and unclasp my eyes,
did I too look at the moon
and drink bowls
of the liquid verb, still and black?
I also kept staring
at the boats and the storks which were leaving
but we women all waited
                              in vain
in tears
for our fathers, loved ones
sons and brothers.
But the city opens wide the jaws
of its prisons
swallows them with its tea
and then fans itself.
But the city pulls its knives
whittles us a body without limbs
a face without a voice
but the city bears its heart
as we do our walls,
but the city . . .
I hurt even down to my shadow cast
upon the other sidewalk
where my latest poems are strewn
in little crystals of opaque salts
like icy tears.
My head falls down on my chest
like a mortar shell
seen from close up, my heart is a lake.

Muhammad 'Abd al–Hayy

(b. 1944)

Born in Sudan, 'Abd al-Hayy was educated in Khartoum and Oxford, where he received a Ph.D. in comparative literature in 1973. He has since been teaching at the University of Khartoum. He has, in addition to works of literary criticism, published collections of poetry, including Return to Sinnar *(1973),* Ode of Signs *(1977), and* The Last Rose Garden. *His poetry avoids the directly political that is a common feature of much comtemporary Arab and African poetries. As Salma Khadra Jayyusi puts it, his poetry "in its terseness of style and power of expression . . . proves to be firmly rooted in the strong poetic tradition of the Sudan."⁴ The following poem was translated from the Arabic by Matthew Sorenson and Alistair Elliot.*

ODE OF SIGNS

I. The Adam Sign

> With Names we summon Cosmos out of Chaos
> Waves Dunes
> Stone Wind Water
> Forest Fire Female
> The Darkness The Lights
>
> And God arrives
> Wearing His holy Names
> Inside the Names
>
> Tonight is the birth of His vision

II. The Noah Sign

Into the face of the Lord I almost scream:
"How could You rest after releasing this
Terrible flood onto the fields we formed
By the sweat of our brow these many arid years,
This crescent of green we pulled out of the jaws
                    of the lion of drought?
                    Why must the wilderness
                    Begin again?"

Instead I shout
As the universe slides into sunset:
"O Lightning! Flash in the darkness of His wrath
And fill my psalm with light:
My ark of weakness and desire
That teems with new birth for our ancient land."

III. The Abraham Sign

Will he come?
Will he come across the night of words?
Across the silence of speech?
Across the starry rose at the center of night?
Bright as the blade of words across the flesh of darkness?

Will he come, your other angel, tonight? Listen!
The cry of a hawk The warning of nature
The frothy blood of a slaughtered lamb in the track of
    heaven
Horse–bodies shining in the clouds
Above the trees and in the wind
The language of green, blazing,
The night–bird in flight
Turns to ashes inside the mirrors of fire.

IV. The Moses Sign

Ashes in virgin morning they collect and rise
As green trees in clear light
As red fruit on the fresh branch
A white bird A generous well

Everything
Is a dream that speaks of the promised land.

V. The Jesus Sign

This is the ringing of dawn's foot
On hills and in the trees
Telling how wind boomed through the grand guitar
How Virgin and angel embraced
In canopies of fire
In street–noise and in dust
How they took leave:
He to his heaven
She to her conquered body
And the song of blood began
That comes to light in the throat of sparrows.

VI. The Muhammad Sign

The garden surprised us
The garden startled us and
At its heart like a rose of fire
The lights converged like silver stallions
In this kingdom without clouds the peacocks
Spread their embroidery
Everything held among the branches of truth
Myrtle of fire A wave in deep seas
Of Flame of Beauty of Fortune
Where the bird falls before it meets the shore
And greets, delighted, its own conflagration.

The garden surprised us
The garden of blossoms bewildered us
At the center shines the green–domed shrine
Good news resounds, loud and sublime
Joy for the birth of the Chosen One
The garden arrayed in the new sunlight
Ecstatic
And the names sang.

VII. A Sign

A sun of grass and two doves singing
Before the beginning and after the end
Of Time
They burn in the branches
Of the transparent willow.

Muhammad al-Ghuzzi

(b. 1949)

Born in the ancient Tunisian city of Qairwan, al-Ghuzzi studied literature at the University of Tunis. He worked as a teacher in his hometown upon graduation. His upbringing in the highly Islamic environment has influenced his poetry. According to Salma Khadra Jayyusi, al-Ghuzzi's collec- tion of poetry, The Book of Water . . . The Book of Embers *(1982), "demonstrates a refreshing new direction away from the often militant verse and loud tones of poetry east of the Mediterranean, and is character- ized by a compact mystical language and a philosophical outlook."*[5] *The three poems below were translated from the Arabic by May Jayyusi and John Heath-Stubbs.*

FEMALE

Do you not see that we pitched our tent on the banks of night
And called out to you to enter in safety
So that we could wash your face at night with sea water,
Your face where ancient terror dwells?
Did you not crave sanctuary of the wind, and we gave you
    shelter?
Did you not tremble and we called to you
To drink our wine from earthen vessels,
That wine whose praises you have sung?
Did we not call upon you to seal in the blue of night
A convenant with the land you seek?
This is your drawn countenance
The water birds enter it in flocks
And this is your house, open,
                    Pledged to the flood-tide of the sea.

The Female called out your name saying:
"Do not betray me, Master,
Descend into my body, cleanse
With night rituals its estrangement;
Of antique cedar wood is our bed,
And full of gladness is the night; be with me."
Why did you lose her, Master? They say she cast
Her girdle and earrings to the waters of the sea,
They say we saw her before people crying out:
"Who of you can restore to me my Master whom I love,
A young man like the cyprus tree, all the birds of evening
Are reflected in the depth of his eyes;
I invited him into my mother's house,
I said do not saddle your horses for the valley of God
That path has no guide and winter is on the roads,
What should you seek?—God is here in my body."

Why did you lose her, Master?
They say we saw her, face to the sea, arms open, calling:
"Come to me now, my body celebrates you."
Why did you lose her, Master? Here you return
Dust on your shoulders, heavily burdened,
In your open face the osprey finds a home.
Descend in safety, let's wash
Your face at night with sea water,
Your face where ancient terror dwells.
Did you not crave sanctuary of the wind, and we gave you
    shelter?
Did you not tremble and we called to you
To drink our wine from earthen vessels,
That wine whose praises you have sung?
Did we not call upon you to seal in the blue of night
A convenant with the land you seek?
This is your drawn countenance
The water birds enter it in flocks
and this is your house, open,
                    Pledged to the flood–tide of the sea.

QUATRAINS FOR JOY

When joy surprises me, I ripen
Before the gathering of figs and grapes,
And call to my master who is one with my soul:
"Pour out your wine for all, my body is the cup."

When joy surprises me, the sea
Floods in upon the thresholds of the night
Carrying in a basket all the fruits of the season
And I make myself a necklace of the sea's treasures.

When joy surprises me, I cry out:
"Master alight at my side,
I will hide you tonight in the cloak of my love,
Here's my body flowering for your wayward stallions."

When joy surprises me, I come forth
with my loosened hair, following my lovers,
I open my breast to the bird flocks, "who," I say,
"Will repair to the regions of the Female if lovers go?"

When joy surprises me, I come forth
From my hidden cities and kindle my incense-burners,
And bless the tree of my body; then all I've hidden
Shows on my face and my secret is out.

When joy surprises me, I inhabit
the incandescent kingdom of lightning
Sleep with the sap in the heart of the leaf,
Return when the palm branch is heavy with dates.

When joy surprises me, I cry out,
"Priest of the Nile Valley, here are my fish
Dead, and my horse is slain before me.
With what chant then shall I open this requiem?"

When joy surprises me, I go
To the soothsayer bearing my broken pitcher
And he lays his hands on my chilled body and declares,
"For seven nights shall this glad face be grieved."

When joy surprises me, I behold
A hawk perched on the castles of the winds
I loosen my locks over my face and cry,
"From what frontiers does this portent come?"

When joy surprises me, and its white gulls
Alight on my body, I see my shroud
Through my ecstasy, and so I strew
All I possess on the waves and I depart.

THE PEN

Take a pen in your uncertain fingers,
Trust, and be assured
That the whole world is a sky–blue butterfly,
and that words are the nets to capture it.

Amina Said

(b. 1953)

⌒

Born in Tunis, Said has published two collections of poetry, titled Paysages,
Nuit Friable *(1980) and* Metamorphose et la Vague *(1985). The four poems
below were translated from the French by Eric Sellin.*

ON THE TATTERED EDGES ...

on the tattered edges of my unravelling memory
heiress of time
the water and sand sing in my veins

before my eyes springs
abundance ringed round by the barest deserts
of your horizonless freedom your prison without bars

you rediscover a destiny
in the figurines born of hard night
many strange things indeed
to search through until a name comes to mind

the madman and his monster
as though they were dying furiously digging
their own graves in the depths of violent sleep

and in the sands of memory
only the tracks of two bodies
and no one notices
the cold enemy
returning calmly
to prowl with the stark morning

they are only whispers
I shall go out under the sun
to sing with the loudest voice

MY WOMAN'S TRANSPARENCE

my woman's transparence
has the whole sea
as its mirror

my sea-spray is born
of the salt of its peaks

my voice plays echo
to its thunder
and to its murmurs

we were
as one sea-swell
when we strode
toward land

we joined hands

THE AFRICA OF THE STATUE

the africa of the statue
flows out in a sawdust
of blood

a split belly
a speckled cosmos
scarified spikes
aslant in the sun

griots discover
that they are the stuff of memory

they bump
in fragments
up against the sky and the shore

and hasten
to rebuild our legends
with their wounded words

the dream of the past
is as a future

THE VULTURES GROW IMPATIENT

1

the vultures grow impatient
with this man between two worlds
counting in his language
the alphabet of passion
the origins of the wind
the long delights
the daylong solitudes
and the secret of others
the stars and their paths
the branchings of coral
and their metamorphoses
the words strung
on the thread of pain
the forgetting of what endures

the anointment of another life
in one's arms
he would seek an abode
in the dizziness of an echo
the presence in the midst of things
of a day as naked as a woman
her spine uncurled
in stormy sleep
the language inherent in bodies

2

in order that our real
place be a place created
we must isolate the vision
of a higher life
that time recede from us
from age to age
that infinity lose sight of us
that the heart the better to understand
become the prey of the world

SOUTHERN AFRICA

Angola
South Africa
Zimbabwe

Joao Pedro

(b. 1948?)

Born in Namibia, Pedro has lived in Luanda, where he works in the ministry of development. He has published a collection of poems titled Ponto de Situação *(1978). Like Jofre Rocha, his poetry is informed by experience of the Angolan liberation war. The following poem was translated from the Portuguese by Don Burness.*

HOMECOMING

Camarada arrived at his village
(the war had ended),
Camarada returned to his village
tired
from war and territory defended.

There was a taste
of salt in his mouth
as he recollected the days of violence.
He wanted to speak.
There was only silence.

This was not the village he saw
when during a lull in the war
resting on the grass
he used to dream of his village.
—It was just his village, nothing more.

Coming home in the maximbombo*
he looked in the eyes of the men
he looked at the faces of the women
he coughed from the exhaust
he paid for his ticket.

Camarada was just like everyone else.
No one noticed him
no one paid attention.

Camarada arrived at his house.
He knocked on the door,
and waited . . .
("please wait a minute camarada").
He saw his family
and he cried . . .

—There was a taste
in his mouth
He was home from the war,
he had not died.

"I have come home"
was all that he said.
Camarada was tired
and lay down on his bed.
The war was not over.

**maximbombo:* bus.

Jofre Rocha

(b. 1951)

Roberto Antonio Victor Francisco de Almeida, using the pen name Jofre Rocha, was born in Icolo e Bengo. After going to school in Luanda, he worked there as a bank clerk. He was arrested after joining the Popular Movement for the Liberation of Angola (MPLA) and jailed until 1968. After Angola won independence in 1975, he became director-general of external relations and later deputy minister, and in 1978 he became minister of external trade. His collection of poems and songs of the people and the revolution, Assim se Fez Madrugada, *was published in 1977. Many of his poems relate to his experience of the MPLA liberation struggle. The two poems below were translated from the Portuguese by Don Burness.*

GUERILLA FIGHTER

I knew a guerilla fighter
small but courageous
who challenged death to combat
and won.
He was small
but in his veins
howitzers of fury
and fire
and his blood was a river
flowing with the salt and honey of victory.

That guerilla fighter
that fearless combatant
is you, my camarada.

POEM OF RETURN

When I return from the land of exile and silence,
do not bring me flowers.

Bring me rather all the dews,
tears of dawns which witnessed dramas.
Bring me the immense hunger for love
and the plaint of tumid sexes in star–studded night.
Bring me the long night of sleeplessness
with mothers mourning, their arms bereft of sons.

When I return from the land of exile and silence,
no, do not bring me flowers . . .

Bring me only, just this
the last wish of heroes fallen at day–break
with a wingless stone in hand
and a thread of anger snaking from their eyes.

Mafika Pascal Gwala

(b. 1946)

Born in Verulam, Natal, Gwala studied politics and industrial relations at the University of Manchester, England. He has worked as an industrial relations officer among black workers, and was a leading exponent of the Black Consciousness Movement in the early 1970s. He has published two collections of poetry, titled Jol'inkomo (Bringing the Cattle Home to the Kraal) in 1977 and No More Lullabies (1982). He has also published a collection of Zulu praise poems titled Musho (1991), with Liz Gunner.

FROM THE OUTSIDE

We buried Madaza
on a Sunday;
big crowd:
hangarounds, churchgoers,
drunks and goofs;
even the fuzz
were there
as the priest
hurried
the burial sermon—
and we filled the grave
with red soil,
the mourning song
pitched fistedly high;
what got my brow itching though
is that none
of the cops present
dared to stand out
and say
Madaza was a "Wanted."

PROMISE!

"At least we can meet at the Indian Market,"
she said way back in Cato Manor.
Haven't met her since.
She, pushed into Umlazi;
Me, pushed into Kwa–Mashu.
She looks at the city from the south;
I descend upon it from the north.
Looks like we've been both lost in the grey
dizziness of our townships. That we can't meet.
OR—who hasn't kept the promise?

Zindzi Mandela

(b. 1959)

Born in South Africa, Zindzi is the younger daughter of Nelson and Winnie Mandela. When still a teenager, she published two collections of poems titled Black as I Am *(1978) and* Black and Fourteen. *She has appeared in many poetry anthologies. Her lyrical poetry resembles the simple, short poems of Langston Hughes and deals with her private experiences and sociocultural issues.*

THERE'S AN UNKNOWN RIVER IN SOWETO

There's an unknown river in Soweto
some say it flows with blood
others say it flows with tears
a leader says
it flows with health and purity
the kind of water
that nobody drinks in Soweto

There's an unknown tree in Soweto
some say it bears sorrow
others say it bears death
a leader says
it bears health and purity
the kind of fruit
that nobody tastes in Soweto

There's an unknown river in Soweto
there's an unknown tree in Soweto
the body
the blood
both unknown

I SAW AS A CHILD

I saw as a child
a small white boy
sitting in a car
and I never knew why
when my home was so far
and his so near
I had to walk

I saw as a child
a tall building
beautiful and empty
and I never knew why
when my home was so small
and this so big
we were overcrowded

I saw as a child
a tarred road
clean and lonely
and I never knew why
when our street was so busy
and this so alone
it was uncared for

I HAVE TRIED HARD

I have tried hard
brother
and I won't give up
even if
that which I cannot see
creeps up behind me
and crushes me to pulp
or even if
that which I cannot see
overtakes me
and leaves me behind
to ponder

   conclude
I have yet to take
another step
and within that time
develop

I WAITED FOR YOU LAST NIGHT

I waited for you last night
I lay there in my bed
like a plucked rose
its falling petals my tears

the sound that my room
   inhaled
   drew in softly
   swallowed
in my ears
was the tapping on the window

getting up
I opened it
and a moth flew in
powdering my neck
shrugging
I caught its tiny wings
and kissed it
I climbed back into bed
with it
and left it to flutter around my head

I waited for you last night

Gcina Mhlophe

(b. 1958)

Born in Hammarsdale, Natal, Mhlophe started writing poems in Xhosa while in high school, and later started writing in English. She is an actress and director and has been involved with the Market Theatre. She has also worked for radio and television. She has participated in the Edinburgh Festival and toured Europe and the United States. She won the Obie Award for her role in Born in the RSA. *In addition to children's tales and short stories, she has published poems in several anthologies.*

SOMETIMES WHEN IT RAINS

Sometimes when it rains
I smile to myself
And think of times when as a child
I'd sit by myself
And wonder why people need clothes

Sometimes when it rains
I think of times
When I'd run into the rain
Shouting "Nkce-nkce mlanjana
When will I grow?
I'll grow up tomorrow!"

Sometimes when it rains
I think of times
When I watched goats
Running so fast from the rain
While sheep seemed to enjoy it

Sometimes when it rains
I think of times
When we had to undress
Carry the small bundles of uniforms and books
On our heads
And cross the river after school

Sometimes when it rains
I remember times
When it would rain hard for hours
And fill our drum
So we didn't have to fetch water
From the river for a day or two

Sometimes when it rains
Rains for many hours without break
I think of people
Who have nowhere to go
No home of their own
And no food to eat
Only rain water to drink

Sometimes when it rains
I think of "illegal" job seekers
In big cities
Dodging police vans in the rain
Hoping for darkness to come
So they can find some wet corner to hide in

Sometimes when it rains
Rains so hard hail joins in
I think of life prisoners
In all the jails of the world
And wonder if they still love
to see the rainbow at the end of the rain

Sometimes when it rains
With hail stones biting the grass
I can't help thinking they look like teeth
Many teeth of smiling friends
Then I wish that everyone else
Had something to smile about.

Luvuyo Mkangelwa

(b. 1977)

Born in Transkei, Mkangelwa moved to Cape Town at the age of nine to live with her mother. She was recently studying personnel management at the Cape Technikon. A promising young poet, she has published poems in magazines, including New Contrast, Carapace, Tribute, *and* RealTime. *Her poetry displays keen insight and freshness.*

OBSERVATIONS

Children play with dolls & toys
others play in mud and dust,

A boy buys sweets & chips,
another begs at subways

A man commands,
another complies

Someone walks, someone rides,
someone drives,
others float as others fly

Some live in cans,
others in mansions

We only breathe the same air,
live in the same planet
& die the same way.

THE WOMEN SING . . .

The women sing
songs of worship
to make their journey
only a step away

The women sing,
banging carriage walls
& whacking their bibles
with their strong hands
for drum–like sounds
The women sing
to conquer the thoughts
of the day's orders

The women sing!
The women sing
to be free!

The women sing
to possess themselves
for a moment
at least!

Christine (Douts) Qunta

(b. 1952)

Born in Kimberly, Qunta gave up studies in the 1970s to work in the black community. She was an executive of the South African Students Organization and the Black People's Convention in the Western Cape. She was forced to leave the country after being detained for her political activities during apartheid. She is currently a practicing solicitor in Zimbabwe. Her poems are published in a collection titled Hoyi Na! Azania—Poems of an African Struggle *(1979), and she edited* Women in Southern Africa *(1987).*

THE KNOW

the know
is in the brown–red broken nipples
of my pregnant breasts
from which the warm milk
will spurt in gleeful dance
the know is written
on the innocent swelling of my hips
the know is in the
majestic black glint in my eye
it is in the pulsating
sometimes lilting tunes
flowing from the sadness in my voice
spilling from oceans of angry waves

the know
lives in sweet–sad gaiety
exuberant utterances of self–pride
viciousness
bitterness
love
enlightenment
the know is in knowing him
better than him knowing me
it is tasting and spitting him out.

Leseko Rampolekeng

(b. 1965)

Born in Soweto, Rampolekeng (also spelled Lesego Rampolokeng) attended the University of the North. He has recited praise poetry at political meetings and performed his poetry with musicians. He has coproduced Faustus in Africa *with William Kentridge and published two collections of poetry,* titled Horns for Hondo *(1990) and* Talking Rain *(1993). His radical and oftentimes shocking poetry shows the influence of performance and music.*

WELCOME TO
THE NEW CONSCIOUSNESS

Welcome to the new consciousness
we utilise everyone

some fertilise the soil
some are food for lies & lice
some's only toil is to BE pigsties
some sit in the power tower
some shit in a flower shower
some cower from hate's gleam in the street
while some meet the NEW DREAM with a scream

the war is done the gore is won
there's something for everyone

for some the sun
for some the moon
for some (perhaps the wise)
both the sun & the moon rise
some take acid moon trips
& some are microwaved in slave ships
some spin in space
while some make the pace of the human race

some hermaphrodites in the light
are eunuchs in the dark
some dicks are sticks some are ticks
some are sick getting their kicks
when the weak lick them slick
some lynch erections
some have ejaculations for lunch
& some count on cunt & cum
while some just read palms & psalms
for a sum of things to come

some are the storm
some the worm
some are only calm
tongue-deep in a bum

some play the death-game
some are too lame for the shame
of this sham-change
some are just deranged small change
while some cringe & some whinge
some are things to give joy
to the uncouth
some are just toyi-toyi boys
throw stones by day
& sow moans by night

some are hypochristians
some are wine–drunken catholics
taking a tumble on the bible
casting a coy look at the prayer-book
while some live in rotten sperm & jackal laughter
some strip to their souls
& show the holes
& some burrow like moles
& if you're hip
you can hop to the top
jump into the mine
& PUMP UP on the drum & bass line

some perverts work on the nerves
some just work on their relatives
some make music
some speak the lyrics
of violence
in tongues of silence

WELCOME to the new consciousness
of derearranged senses
we utilise everyone

WET PAIN . . . TREAD WITH CARE

tattered rain
& i'm navy blue
in the frayed streets
pressure reaching down
& slow magic coming on
drum flute & the night whistle
mute music of torn throats

& then . . .
tongues twisted around on themselves
spew out froth
green
rabid at yellow dusk . . .

& the night gathers its red soaked apparel
staggers home

Mongane Wally Serote

(b. 1944)

Serote was born in Sophiatown, a Johannesburg township that was destroyed under apartheid. He was detained for nine months under the Terrorism Act in 1969–1970 and was released without trial. After earning an M.F.A. in creative writing from Columbia University, he worked in Gaberone, Botswana. He later worked in the Department of Arts and Culture of the UK office of the African National Congress. Currently a member of the South African Parliament, Serote is both chairman of its Portfolio Committee for Arts, Culture, Language, Science, and Technology and head of the ANC Department of Arts and Culture in Johannesburg. He has published a novel and five collections of poetry—Yakhal'inkomo (The Cry of Cattle at the Slaughterhouse) *in 1972,* Tsetlo (Honey-bird) *in 1974,* No Baby Must Weep *(1975),* Behold Mama, Flowers, *and* Third World Express *(1992). A leading figure of the new African poetry, his poetry captures the plight of Africans in the apartheid period and is not only the most intensely engaged of the young South African poets but also part of the revival of black writing in the 1970s.*

OFAY–WATCHER LOOKS BACK

I want to look at what happened;
That done,
As silent as the roots of plants pierce the soil
I look at what happened,
Whether above the houses there is always either smoke or dust,
As there are always flies above a dead dog.
I want to look at what happened.

That done,
As silent as plants show colour: green,
I look at what happened,
When houses make me ask: do people live there?
As there is something wrong when I ask—is that man alive?
I want to look at what happened.
That done,
As silent as the life of a plant that makes you see it
I look at what happened
When knives creep in and out of people
As day and night into time.
I want to look at what happened,
That done,
As silent as plants bloom and the eye tells you:
                        something has happened.
I look at what happened.
When jails are becoming necessary homes for people
Like death comes out of disease,
I want to look at what happened.

CITY JOHANNESBURG

This way I salute you:
My hand pulses to my back trousers pocket
Or into my inner jacket pocket
For my pass, my life,
Jo'burg City.
My hand like a starved snake rears my pockets
For my thin, ever lean wallet,
While my stomach groans a friendly smile to hunger,
Jo'burg City.
My stomach also devours coppers and papers
Don't you know?
Jo'burg City, I salute you;
When I run out, or roar in a bus to you,
I leave behind me, my love
My comic houses and people, my dongas and my ever whirling
    dust,
My death,
That's so related to me as a wink to the eye.
Jo'burg City
I travel on your black and white and roboted roads,
Through your thick iron breath that you inhale,
At six in the morning and exhale from five noon.
Jo'burg City
That is the time when I come to you,
When your neon flowers flaunt from your electrical wind,
That is the time when I leave you,
When your neon flowers flaunt their way through the falling
    darkness
On your cement trees.
And as I go back, to my love,
My dongas, my dust, my people, my death,
Where death lurks in the dark like a blade in the flesh
I can feel your roots, anchoring your might, my feebleness
In my flesh, in my mind, in my blood,
And everything about you says it,
That, that is all you need of me.
Jo'burg City, Johannesburg
Listen when I tell you

There is no fun, nothing, in it,
When you leave the women and men with such frozen
    expressions,
Expressions that have tears like furrows of soil erosion,
Jo'burg City, you are dry like death,
Jo'burg City, Johannesburg, Jo'burg City.

ALEXANDRIA

Were it possible to say,
Mother, I have seen more beautiful mothers,
A most loving mother,
And tell her there I will go,
Alexandria, I would have long gone from you.

But we have only one mother, none can replace,
Just as we have no choice to be born,
We can't choose mothers;
We fall out of them like we fall out of life to death.

And Alexandria,
My beginning was knotted to you,
Just like you knot my destiny.
You throb in my inside silences
You are silent in my heart-beat that's loud to me.
Alexandria often I've cried.
When I was thirsty my tongue tasted dust,
Dust burdening your nipples.
I cry Alexandria when I am thirsty.
Your breasts ooze the dirty waters of your dongas,
Waters diluted with the blood of my brothers, your children,
Who once chose dongas for death-beds.
Do you love me Alexandria, or what are you doing to me?

You frighten me, Mama,
You wear expressions like you would be nasty to me,
You frighten me, Mama,
when I lie on your breast to rest, something tells me,
You are bloody cruel.
Alexandria, hell
What have you done to me?
I have seen people but I feel like I'm not one,
Alexandria what are you doing to me?

I feel I have sunk to such meekness!
I lie flat while others walk on me to far places.
I have gone from you, many times,
I come back.
Alexandria, I love you;
I know
when all these worlds became funny to me,
I silently waded back to you
and amid the rubble I lay,
Simple and black.

THIS OLD WOMAN

This old woman, stalking up the street,
Is an old knitted jersey now,
Worn and torn
By her children, children's children,
And nowadays, children of boys and girls.
She unfolds,
As though from her woven pouches,
Beauty foreign to me;
Me talking with her,
I feel the bitter winter cold;
It's like driving in a car
Watching untouched natural scenery unfold
(Me think angrily rushing past, the car windows remaining
    behind).
And when I stop and think,
the prize: a frozen past.
This old woman stalks up the street now
Like the stranger that takes a glance at me
From his car, and me from mine,
When the traffic light turns: Red!
This old woman.

Samuel Chimsoro

(b. 1949)

Trained as a laboratory technician, Chimsoro works in a government radiation detection laboratory. His poetry appears in several anthologies and his published collection of poetry is titled Smoke and Flames.

THE CURFEW BREAKERS

to walk in the sun
hoe in hand,
to dig drains
and engrave sorrow
on anthills
is for the love of life.

to sweep the streets
and fence the gates,
to keep next of kin informed that
the right of admission
into the sun
is reserved
is for the love of life.

to turn to moonlight
for reflections of warmth,
to dance to drums
barefooted
and sanctify the earth
as the dust of ancestors
is freed from the earth
is for the love of life.

to sleep
on the skeletons
of fallen stars
and dream that
the right of admission
into the darkness
is reserved
is for the love of life.

to wake up in the morning
as an object of dispute
and die in the evening
as a curfew breaker
is also for the love of life.

THE CHANGE

What used to be
A missionary's poker
Is now a scepter
Leaning against a sooted chimney.
The soft white wood
Has all burnt.
Its reluctant warmth is refuse
Diffused into the earth;
The grey covering ashy trash
Wanting to be blown.
What used to be
A gregarious row of chairs,
Docks and electric seats
Is now a row of stone
Round an outdoor fireplace
Loaded with mutsatsati logs.
The heat of riots is gone.
The heart of sermons is gone.
Speeches were concluded
Now speakers are redundant.
What used to be
So white is now all
In the museum of memory
While black hands dip
Lumps of their constitution
In the same soup bowl.

Chenjerai Hove

(b. 1956)

A Zimbabwean poet and novelist, Hove has published collections of poetry and fiction, including Up in Arms *(1982),* Swimming in Floods of Tears *(1983),* Red Hills of Home *(1985),* Masimba Avanhu *(1986),* Bones *(1988), and* Shadows *(1991). His fictional* Bones *won the Noma Prize in 1989.*

RED HILLS OF HOME

Father grew up here
tuning his heart
to the sound of the owl from the moist green hills;
beyond, the eagle swam in the air
while mother–ant dragged
an unknown victim to a known hole
printed on the familiar unreceding earth.

I grew up here,
father died underground seven rainless seasons ago
and the burial news
was all we had to bury.
Now the featherless eagle, like roast meat,
recites the misery of the dusty sky.
Mother–ant never surfaces
for father is enough meat, underground.
The green hills of home died,
Red hills cut the sky
and the nearby sooty homes of peasants
live under the teeth of the roaring bulldozer.
Yesterday sabhuku Manyonga had the push
of muscular hands on his chest
and now lives in drunken exile.

Red hills have come
with wounds whose pus
suffocates the peasant.
The peasant's baby sleeps
knowing only thin dreams of a moonlight joy.
Dying too are the songs
of the seasons that father once sang
Red hills and the smoke of man–made thunder
plunder the land under contract.
If father rose from the dead
he would surely not know
the very ant–hill embracing his blood
buried with the umbilical cord.
Here, on this bit of ground
earth once lay pregnant
but now
the sacred hill bleeds
robbed even of her decent name,
her holy cows are milked
by hunger–laden hands
whose mouths eat man
gulped down by this eerie giant's throat
sitting where once you flowed
with calm holy water.

Red hills and the smell of exile;
Chipo died this morning
no more burial song ripped the air
nor do we feel safe to bury her
knowing tomorrow a bulldozer comes
to scatter these malnourished bones.

Red hills, and the smell of exile
Exile breathing over our shoulder
in a race that already looks desperate.
Red hills, and the pulse of exile
telling us this is home no more.

YOU WILL FORGET

If you stay in comfort too long
you will not know
the weight of a water pot
on the bald head of the village woman

You will forget
the weight of three bundles of thatch grass
on the sinewy neck of the woman
whose baby cries on her back
for a blade of grass in its eyes

Sure, if you stay in comfort too long
you will not know the pain
of child birth without a nurse in white

You will forget
the thirst, the cracked dusty lips
of the woman in the valley
on her way to the headman who isn't there

You will forget
the pouring pain of a thorn prick
with a load on the head.
If you stay in comfort too long

You will forget
the wailing in the valley
of women losing a husband in the mines.

You will forget
the rough handshake of coarse palms
full of teary sorrow at the funeral.

If you stay in comfort too long
You will not hear
the shrieky voice of old warriors sing
the songs of fresh stored battlefields.

You will forget
the unfeeling bare feet
gripping the warm soil turned by the plough

You will forget
the voice of the season talking to the oxen.

Dambudzo Marechera

(1954-1987)

Born in Zimbabwe, Marechera lived in both England and Zimbabwe. He first came into prominence with his book of short stories, The House of Hunger *(1978). A vibrant personality, he shunned conventions. Many of his works were published posthumously by F. Veit-Wild. Marechera's works include* The Black Insider *(1990),* Cemetery of Mind *(1992), and* Scrapiron Blues *(1994). There is lyrical intensity and a feeling of desperation and loss, especially in the poems in* Cemetery of Mind *that he wrote while sick and approaching untimely death.*

DESERT CROSSING

Sharp howling winds scattering grit
Crack and roar like creatures of the pit:
The heart is a desert place, an earth of piercing heat.

The burning sky above is fixed,
The consuming grave at our feet baffles the priest;
Day after day the sand–dunes of living shift about,
Creeping forever across the desert's immense minute.

THE OLD MAN INSIDE ME

The old man inside me
Wants to shred my face,
The chicken to crack the shell,
History to havoc present illusions.

Patches of dead skin on my hands
Announce the divine imminence,
Rags of dour clouds sour my optimism
Storms of silent wrath turn into poems.

I cannot forgive youth
Yet would forget old age
I waver between light & dark
& fight certainty with uncertainty.

I am a table made miraculously by stray
Cigarette burns & stains of holy wine;
The old gambler plays early and late
This game of chance for a pyrrhic memorial.

WHEN LOVE'S PERISHED

Here comes one who in silence
Howled a thousand torments;
One who behind polite phrases
Screamed terrible curses to the sky;
One whose slow measured pace to the altar
Raised more dust than buffalo stampeding—
The soft sweaty palm in limpid handshake
Hid a grizzly bear's hairy powerful claws.
But the mirror impassively denied it all.
The poem, sticky with centuries' sleep
And anaemic from lack of iron discipline
And pallid from years' diet of political slogans
And wedged under the door between Europe and Africa,
The poem, in consternation, began to pick its stanza-lips.

THE CEMETERY IN THE MIND

In the kitchen a tangled fetid forest
Through which I hack a path to the sink's shimmering pool;
Depraved crocodiles leer and grunt at my amorous approach;
And from the frothing depths of passion's fury
Suddenly, all above, the magnesium sun bursts into flames.
Plato's teatowels wrap themselves around my brain,
The cockroaches like extincts suddenly resurrected
Flop out of my ears, eyes, nose, arse, onto the primeval floor.
I return to the bedsitting-room ghosts, their lecherous
Silence wrapped in the bright humanskin lampshade,
Their all-knowing glances swivelling to welcome me—
Without pause I strip off my tattered mortality
And, with a crooked smilesigh, sink onto her phantom bosom:
Why O why my Amelia!—and not one of those diseased
      City whores.

NEITHER INNOCENCE
NOR EXPERIENCE

A sudden blow! And she claims me for child
Hawk eye and beard proclaim parenthood over me
Whispering ghosts arrive bearing gifts
Declaring an uncle, an aunt, a sister.
Where am I? Who are these? No sooner arrived
Than I am washed, swaddled, offered swollen breasts.
What a world for a defenceless child!
Then more of them wet me at the fount
Sit me at school desk, propel me to office desk
Till in utter bewilderment I surrender, bite the bit,
And haul me along to the cold anonymous Out There.
What a world for a defenceless youth!
Love surprises my heart at sight of another like me
We wed, drag into light several shrieking children
Who fearfully accept my puzzled fatherhood
And as they grow through th'injustice of it all
Giggle at my dotage, sign me into The Old People's Home
Where now I pen this vague protest, knowing
There is never time to know what is going on.

Kristina Rungano

(b. 1963)

Born in Zimbabwe, Rungano attended Roman Catholic elementary and high schools in Zvimba. She then went to Britain, where she obtained a diploma in computer science. She returned to Zimbabwe in 1982 to work for the Science Computing Centre in Harare. Her poems are published in a collection titled A Storm Is Brewing. *Many of her poems, written when she was about eighteen years old, express nostalgia for traditional African life.*

THIS MORNING

This morning I visited the place where we lay
like animals
O pride be forgotten
And how the moon bathed our savage nudity in purity
And your hands touched mine in a silken caress
And our beings were cleansed as though by wine.
Then you stroked my breast
And through love I shed the tears of my womb
O sweet fluid spilled in the name of love
O love
O sweet of mine existence
Your sigh of content as your lips touched my soul
O joy shared by the wilderness
O gentle breeze
O fireflies that hovered over our nest in protective harmony
How I yearn
I feel you here again with me.

See how the flowers, the grass, even the little shrubs have
    bloomed
Even as I bloomed under the warmth of your breath
And now they look at me; unashamed
For they have been washed and watered by the love of your loins
I stretch and sigh in warm contemplation
For tonight I shall again possess you
In me, I shall be content of all you render
On account of love
Under the stars I shall drink the whisperings of your body
Speak again to the depths of my sensibility
Tree of my life
Peaceful meadows
Cow dares not moo here
Ruler of the night
Lord dynamo
Let me not disturb your peace
But let me lie with you again
Be silent O silence
Love has found its awakening

Musaemura Zimunya

(b. 1949)

After completing his graduate studies at Kent University, England, Zimunya returned to Zimbabwe, where he teaches in the English Department of the University of Zimbabwe. He coedited, with Mudereri Kadhani, the anthology And Now the Poets Speak. *He has published a collection of his poems titled* Thought-Tracks *(1982). In his poems, he tells sarcastic and humorous stories, which indicate a certain nostalgia for the traditional, rural way of life.*

ARRIVANTS

They came back home from bush–haunts
and refugee camps the living and the dead;
they flew back from misery's northern coldness
and humiliation's faithful missionaries abroad
to colours, bunting, pennants and earthborn songs
that awoke History and tradition with a bang–bang.

Came to Hope–dawns and democracy with strings attached
and so we were reconciled to white faces
whose pride and heads had watered UDI and racism—
aren't they keen to teach us compassion!

The year sped on caterpillar wheels as a result
but our ninety–year old patience seemed to have endless reach
so we could still listen to the critics of our monthly
emigration statistics without wishing for another Ben–Bella.

Then, also, Bulawayo was a place of killing again
to remind us that our peace was a hasty marriage
where we had no training camps for the new order—
to say that the power of peace must in the new age
reside in hearts of Ndebele and Shona, not in gun–barrels.

Yet when quiet returned in the area of madness
Chaminuka's words came torrenting and torrenting
and seriously we wondered who would stop this Rain,
or dare we murder another *mhondoro**?

Or dare we have more petals of blood simply
because someone's whim pleads for more petals of blood
tomorrow and tomorrow when most want life and rest?
We, indeed, are arrivants with blister–feet and broken bones
that will learn the end of one journey
begins another.

**mhondoro:* Shona for spirit-medium.

KISIMISO

The family were gathered
the eldest son from Bulawayo
boastful of his experiences in the city of knives and crooks;
one son from Harare,
a fish-pocket who slang everyone
into ignorance with the stupefying *s'kuz'apo** tongue
(the family believe he is the chief mechanic at Lever Brothers!);
a sister, latest to arrive, from Gutu
blue-painted eye-lids, false eye-lashes, red lips
bangles gritting in her hands
with a European hair-wig above an Ambi-proof face
she covers her thighs with a towel when she sits
(as for her the family will always believe she is a
dressmaker in Ft. Vic); the rest of the family, mum
and dad, are happy to admire the latest from town.

Kisimiso means feasting
dozens of bread loaves, drums of tea, mountains of *sadza*
rock-size pieces of meat of the he-goat
in lakes of thousand-eyed soup
and, of course, large pots of fizzing frothy beer.
Nothing about the print themes of good will and peace
of course good will was always here;
an old man well-known to me lost half his hair
while pulling a tourist out of a blazing car wreckage—in June,
six moons before last Christmas.

**s'kuz'apo:* urban slang for "excuse-me there."

A child without clothes sat nodding with sleep,
his belly as big as a *muchongoyo** drum:
buzzing flies were fighting, spinning and tumbling
into the smelling parting between his buttocks,
Kutu the scraggy dog was retching in front of him;
they ultimately gave the mother water that
had washed the madman's beard
because she could no longer leave the bush
or close her oozing behind
and brother *s'kuz'apo*
filled the boys' hut with urine and vomit
and a powerful smell of beer gone stale.

The next day
they talked of the greatest Kisimiso
for many years.

**muchongoyo:* Shona for a vibrant traditional dance.

LET IT BE

Frelimo Oya
Frelimo Oya
Frelimo yagoya

O God
Let it be
You were there when the detainee
was whisked away from his home
on the dark morning;
when his children, his wife
and the servant were locked up at the
Camp for being part of him.
You were there with the detainee,
neck–deep in the dark water cell.
You were there when the bomb
dropped on the half–naked
dust–bellied children
screaming joyfully after each other
playing with dry stalks of maize in the field,
pointing at the roaring 'copter.
(The security forces thought they were guerrillas.)
Yes, weren't you there,
when gelignite exploded in the ears
of these who did not know
where the terrorists were?
Now, then, at Wiriamu,
Lord, I know you were there.
Say it,
say you were there,
you saw the agony of all
and let it be freedom now.
Let it be—freedom.
Amen.

MR BEZUIDENHOUT'S DOGS

Job-seeker, this time hoping
that bwana's warning signs about
dogs and no-jobs would prove untrue
I stood and waited with prickly nerves
and hot awe as yapping jaws locked
on steel with dental impact
at the meshed gate of his suburban house.

Mr Bezuidenhout's dogs have hyena blood
and they howl and bark at everything black,
including shadows, just like RF* backbenchers
during the nth reading of the Land Apportionment
Act (1933) or the Situpa Bill.

---

*RF: Rhodesia Front.

WEST AFRICA

Cameroon
Cape Verde
Côte d'Ivoire
Gambia
Ghana
Guinea
Niger
Nigeria
Senegal
Sierra Leone

Fernando D'Almeida

(b. 1955)

A native of Douala, D'Almeida is a versatile writer and journalist who works for the national newspaper the Cameroon Tribune. *He has published four collections of poetry, including* Au Seuil de l'Exile, En Attendant le Verdit, *and* L'Espace de la Parole. *His poetry deals with daily challenges the individual faces at home and in the work place. The following poem was translated from the French by Faustine Boateng Gyima.*

BY FORTY–SIXTH

So many times
I walked and walked
Following orders
But all is futile
I approached the man
who loiters along the quay
In search of real life
I was not to blame
If to blame is to be lost
In the network of insignificant things
I played the game to discover myself
I told my childhood love
I drank to the health of life
I laughed at my reassuring ignorance

I looked into things
Things were revealed to me
while I reconciled my life
With the life of others
I didn't hide my face
In swaddling clothes of infamy
I passionately uttered an equivocal yes

I am aware of my crazy life
I have reasons for my madness
I didn't reach out to others
Except to be human myself
I am standing firm
As I keep my stand
I shall not let myself be battered by doubt.
I am as secured as Fire.

Gahlia Gwangwa'a

Born in Bali-Nyonga, Gwangwa'a attended school in Douala in then West Cameroon. While in the police force, he took correspondence courses for the General Certificate of Education at Ordinary and Advanced Levels. He later studied in the United States at Widener University, Morgan State University, and Johns Hopkins University, where he obtained a Ph.D. in international business administration. He is a laureate of the National Book Development Council's Literary Contest (1995). He is currently the manager of services in the Personnel Department of Pecten Cameroon Company, and president of the Creative Writers Club of Douala. He has published a collection of poems titled Cry of the Destitute *(1995).*

LEAKING ROOF

You said I could talk
When deep down
You knew no one could
Cough or smile

Your roof is leaking
The bamboos would soon
Give way because of rain water.
Destruction is not far
As the walls are continuously soaked.

By your dictates,
Nothing I say means good.
Your reprisals continue
For fear I wear your shoes
And eat your meals.
I'm unarmed and voiceless.

Nonetheless, listen to
What I have to say
Even if you do nothing about
What I say.

Allow me to say what I think.
I have more things in mind
Which are constructive.
They are not destructive as
You believe every utterance to be.
Your roof is leaking and needs
Immediate mending;
Act now before it's
Too late to do anything.

Your house has imminent ruin
In sight
Leave me to say it.
Others also have better ideas
But won't speak out 'cause
They have no courage.

Open the doors, let others
Listen to what I have to say
They would mend the leaking roof

Do it now or never
When the house is in ruins
There will be no roof to mend.

Sim Kombem

(b. 1962)

Born in Belo-Kom, Kombem received a B.A. in English and literature from the University of Yaoundé. He received an M.A. from Jackson State University and a Ph.D. in mass communications from Howard University. He currently teaches at Florida Memorial College and St. Thomas University in the Washington, D.C., area. In addition to a novel, he has published two poetry collections, Sim's Poetic Column *and* A Bush of Voices.

ANOTHER MOMENT

I
stand alone
eager to hate the guts
you used in wooing a virgin who longed for
the chalk of civilization scratched all over her.
Your little poems, false ramblings
In gin bottles,
Your strange feelings for her, those framed words
of yours faked as affection that have destroyed older girls,
haunt her now like a benign rabbit on a hot summer noon,
panting under stale breath; her little eyes burning;
her fresh bosom sizzling under your large body;
her mind dancing, fiddling to discover you;
her nude self coiling and closing before you
kill me slowly like AIDS.

If I die
I will weather countless thunderstorms
and lightnings, sufficient to burn your thicket.
But if I have wronged the world
If I have spelled love upside down,
If I have dug trenches for escape duikers, or
for lost lambs fleeing from the flames of wild bush fires
O please forgive,
you little lambs leaning up on sleeping lions,
basking under summer sun with leopards.
With cold ashes of love shaking from a gentle breeze, single
do
I
stand
eager to pound my name,
to watch the silhouettes of an early affection pine out
beneath my steady gaze
to read my revelries before they fade behind twilight clouds,
to hatch my egg–dreams before they crack.

Adelina da Silva

(b. 1958)

Born on the island of Fogo in Cape Verde, da Silva migrated to the United States at the age of eighteen. She currently lives and teaches in Roxbury, Massachusetts. Her poems have been published in the journal Arquipelago. "Return to the Homeland" was translated from the Portuguese by Gerald M. Moser. "Along the Banks of the Charles" was translated from the Portuguese by Don Burness.

RETURN TO THE HOMELAND

I feel like a stranger
amidst these bare rocks
only yesterday walls
of a wretched cabin
that had been my home.
Step after step
along your beaches
a child's dim shape
continues walking
which at your breast
saw the light of day.
I'm hearing laughter,
a whisper
come, touch me,
feel me
we're one.

What I'm hearing is not
the voice of yore
the bond that bound me
is slipping I feel it
the sea's tender touches
the breeze bringing coolness
the warm shade of home!
How strange to feel like a prodigal son!

ALONG THE BANKS OF THE CHARLES

Dawn comes and with it nostalgia
There is no moonlight no serenade.
Slowly I go out into the street
to the sound of a chant that has been calling me for a long time.
I leave behind the cold bed
that night after night
receives my secrets.
The quiet street follows my steps,
The proud river becomes sad
and the two of us in somnabulent rhythm
continue on.
In the high sky there are no lights
and not a single image is reflected
in the wide mirror that accompanies me.
The dream has vanished and with it my fantasies.
The wind caresses my face,
my mind tries to capture another
while I go on aimlessly accompanied by
the murmur of the water and the cry of the sea–gull.

Alberto Ferreira Gomes

(b. 1957)

Gomes was born in Mindelo, on the island of São Vicente, Cape Verde. A meteorologist by profession, his poems have been published in Terra Nova. *The following poem was translated from the Portuguese by Gerald M. Moser.*

THE MARTYRED TAMARIND

Under that tamarind tree
A martyr of drought
A martyr of long dry years
Just like its countrymen

Under that tamarind tree
Mistreated by children
Mistreated by us, the children
With ropes to swing on
With stones thrown at it
By breaking its young green shoots
By picking its unripe fruit
Mother Jijulia would sit there
Looking so old and mistreated by life's rough moments
Glad for the shade and the scent of the old tamarind
Old and bent and resistant

But now the tamarind is no more
And Mother Jijulia neither . . .

The tamarind tree that resisted the drought
Was helpless before the man with the axe
Down it went into the fire to cook the *cachupa* . . .
And the children
Who came after us they have no such tree
They have none to give them its shade
They have no tamarind tree to gather its fruit
They have no kindly old Mother Jijulia . . .

Death has taken Mother Jijulia away when she was too old
And man on his own took the tamarind tree
The old tamarind, so resistant, so strong, so good and so . . .
                                    beautiful . . .

Luis Andrade Silva

(b. 1943)

⟵‾‾‾‾‾‾‾‾

Born in Mindelo, Cape Verde, Silva emigrated to France in 1968. He founded the first Cape Verdean Association in Paris and directs the Center for Information for Emigrant Workers in Paris. His poems have appeared in Morabeza, Terra Nova, *and* Arquipelago. *In his poetry, common themes are the dilemma of living abroad and the postcolonial relationship between Cape Verde and Europe. The following poem was translated from the Portuguese by Don Burness.*

THE ISLAND AND EUROPE

To Luiz Romano

From the Island to Europe
We have journeyed chasing dreams of freedom
And money to buy cachupa to feed our families.

Freedom, I well remember, we used to say
Lay beyond the Pyrenees
And money for cachupa, that
Was found over the sea.

And we Cape Verdeans, eternal seafarers,
Would conquer our dreams with the fruit of our labor.

We planned on returning as soon as possible for our final task;
—To confront government clerks, the police,
That entire mob that suck dry our motherland.

THE EMIGRANT'S SON

That thin little boy
Bundled up to protect himself
From the rain and the snow
Black smock
Frail body
Moth eaten beret pulled over his head
And hands in his pockets—
He's an immigrant.

He speaks French
He knows the history of Napoleon
He has read Sartre and Teilhard de Chardin.

Nevertheless, he would like to know something of his country. . .
Each day he must face the racism of his schoolmates,
and ask himself why he must live in this country!
His parents, exhausted from hard daily struggle
Deflect his questions with a simple look of sadness
They hope to return home next year on holiday
And to do so they must work sixteen hours a day.

If God wills, he'll go too!
If only his thin little body
        Can survive
           Winter
               Racism
                    and other miseries! . . .

Veronique Tadjo

(b. 1955)

Born in Côte d'Ivoire, Tadjo has published a collection of poems, Laterite, *which was awarded a literary prize by L'Agence de Cooperation Culturelle et Technique in 1983. She has also published two novels,* A Vol d'Oiseau *(1986) and* Le Royaume Aveugle *(1991). Her poems have appeared in numerous anthologies. She currently teaches in the English Department of the University of Abidjan. Her poems are generally untitled and capitalized throughout. The three poems below were translated from the French by Faustine Boateng Gyima.*

THREE POEMS

LIFE IS MADE
OF BLACK THISTLES AND THORNS
I WOULD HAVE LIKED IT
SWEETER AND LESS BITTER
BUT YOU KNOW
THE LIMIT OF THINGS
SETS BACK EACH MOMENT
OUR FACES CHANGE
AND LOVERS OPPRESS
ONE ANOTHER
YOU KNOW VERY WELL
IN THE NIGHT OF YOUR TERROR
THERE WILL ONLY BE YOU

*   *   *

OVER THERE, PEOPLE
LIVE WITH MANY MANY SECRETS
AND THE BREATH OF GRASSLANDS
WHISTLES ALONG THE ROAD
INTERTWINED WITH PATHS,
THE GREY SKY BECOMES BLUE
AND THE FLUTE THAT YOU HEAR
COMES DIRECTLY
FROM PORO

*   *   *

HE IS MY SHADOW
MY STEP–BY–STEP
MY FURTIVE GLANCE
HE IS MY MAYBE
MY NEWBORN DESIRE
HE IS MY STRENGTH
AND MY WEAKNESS
THE WATER WHICH CARRIES ME
AND THE WATER WHICH DROWNS ME
HE IS WHERE I'D LIKE TO GO
TOMORROW AS WELL AS YESTERDAY

Tijan M. Sallah

(b. 1958)

Born in Sere Kunda, Sallah was educated in the United States, where he obtained a Ph.D. in economics. He has worked as an audit clerk in his native Gambia and has taught at Virginia Polytechnic Institute, Kutztown University, and North Carolina A&T State University, Greensboro. He currently works at the World Bank in Washington, D.C. In addition to a collection of short stories, Before the New Earth, *he has published three collections of poetry—*When Africa Was a Young Woman *(1980),* Kora Land *(1989), and* Dreams of Dusty Roads *(1993)—and edited* New Poets of West Africa *(Malthouse, Lagos, 1995). The leading voice in the new Gambian poetry, Sallah's poems are simple, pungent, and highly imagistic.*

THE ELDERS ARE GODS

In my hometown, there is rust
and shine and kinfolks
Who use the privilege of age
To guarantee their ear of corn.
The old folks say that
If you eat fish–heads, or
Drink coconut juice, you would
Turn stupid. But the elders
Eat everything and
Get wiser everyday.
They set ambiguous rules.
They wall us from corn–filled places.
They say sex is bad for children;
Yet do it in the dark confines
Of their isolated bedrooms.
They say that courtesy is
Good for youth, and palmwine
Bad for their livers.

The elders are gods.
They sit on top of everything.
They tell us that farmwork
Is a good discipline for youth,
That dragging ignorant sheep flocks
To meandering windfields
and tying them on the guava–stumps
Is a good endurance test.
The elders are gods.
They sit on top of the branches.
They have eyes wide as owls'.
They rotate them to every corner.
They want us to follow
Their bygone norms.
They want us never
To put up a fight.
The elders are gods.
They sit on top of everything.

NO ARGUMENT TONIGHT

I would not argue with you tonight
Over salty food and half–cooked rice
For the moon is too hostile,
And I do not want to add
To the madness of this hour.
I would just eat cassava
And fried plantain
And watch the geckoes
Wriggle on the cinder–coated walls
Of our patient kitchen,
While the glittering fireflies
Teach you
The silent grace of marriage.

MR. AGAMA

In our backyard, the agama,
Naturally clothed in crocodile–skin,
Pied–yellow on an ashy background,
Wriggles, namby–pamby.
His grips, so glued to the mango–trunk.

Mr. Agama,
      With your yellow spotted bowtie,
      You look so officious, inscrutable,
      Unfeigning.

The delicacy to your manners,
Like that of the schoolboy
Who feigns affection.
Your body, like wad, is
Slender and elongated.
You, kin to the chameleon;
Yet not clothed in hypocrisy.

Mr. Agama,
      So exacting are your eyes,
      Those marble–balls you rotate
      Like a camera.

Your magnetic tongue,
To insect and flies
It is the subjective inferno.

You, so sober in demeanor;
Yet wily and untutored
When confronted with prey.

Your teeth, tartar–streaked,
Celebrate the rain
And the paroxysm of fly–laughter
Under street lamps.

Mr. Agama,
    Tête–a–tête, with your
    Self–indulgence,
    You tread on unawares.

Know Mr. Agama
That the mango stem,
Wart–like, is no guide
To the certain prey.
It too indulges in the
Treachery game.
So calm, the mango stem stands,
But so aggressive its branches
Traduce you, bargain for you
With the hide–seek monkey,
Or the wicked bush–cat
In exchange for your carcass,
Manure–feed for its roots.

Mr. Agama,
    Pied–yellow and proud,
    Beware of other selves,
    Lurking to strike;
    Other bowtied–selves,
    Officious, inscrutable,
    And unfeigning.

TELEVISION AS GOD

In America, television is a special god
With its priests and priestesses.
No one has time for conversation, or
For each other. Television works
In the remote crania of
Every high–class pleasure.

And the daisies by my apartment–window,
Tall, yellow, as the fingers of the sun,
Why are they so sad from neglect?
They perhaps lost the competition.
Television has trapped everyone
In its shrine.

And the young pour libations
to the sacred ancestors in Hollywood,
And the babies learn their words
Even before they know how to crawl.
And television has its lull, its lilt
And its lure; and the elders
Seat themselves comfortably.
The sedentary god accumulates lard
Between their immobile hips.

And the children say—
How about Eddie Murphy,
Ain't he great?
And sweet Madonna,
Ain't she sexy?

And the mothers wonder
Why their kids are doing poorly in school
And their grammar is as good as chimpanzees'.
And, of course, television is a special god
And gods have their sacred abode
In the hearts of their humble servants.
And television is a god that speaks
And smiles and acts
And emotions are fortified
As starch to ironed clothes.
And the truth of the world is accessed
Through the superficial words
Of the interpreters.

And it is no wonder,
The holy highs of television
Are good friendly waiters, catering
To the standard heart
Of the empire of faith-seekers.

And the thrill is always there
In the ecstasy of Hollywood-preachers.
As the catholic television-watcher put it—
Pope Johnny Carson,
How loaded be thy name.
Die KingKong come.
Thy wisdom be done on earth,
As it is in high-visions.

And its priests and priestesses
Glint with gold and diamonds.
Then the gospels follow,
Sermons to arch-god of Epicurus.

In America, television is a god;
Therapeutic to ailing hearts
As happiness, redemptive
To the eyes as an apocalypse.

Kobena Eyi Acquah

(b. 1951?)

Born in Winneba, Acquah studied at the University of Ghana and the Ghana Law School. He is currently the chief legal adviser to the Bank for Housing and Construction in Accra. He has served in different positions in the Ghana Association of Writers and has been on the executive board of the Ghana Book Development Council. He has also served as a member of Ghana's 1979 Constituent Assembly. His two poetry collections are The Man Who Died *(1985) and* Music for a Dream Dance *(1989). Acquah has won many awards, including the University of Ghana's Langston Hughes Prize (1974), the Valco Fund Literary Award (1977), the Commonwealth Poetry Prize for the Africa Region (1985), and the Ghana Book Award (1986). Acquah's poetry has lyrical strength in its simplicity.*

I WANT TO GO TO KETA

I want to go to Keta
before it's washed away,
before the palm trees wither
and drown outside the bay.

I want to go to Keta
where boys drum all the day
and the girls dance *agbadza*
to keep the tears away.

I want to go to Keta
while yet they live who care
to point out like a star
that frothing spot out there

where they would sit with *dada*
those days the sea was land.
I want to go to Keta
while yet there's place to stand.

I want to go to Keta
before the tenderness
of grief so keen and bitter
chills to cold callousness

and the vagueness of laughter
drowns the shared joy of pain.
I want to go to Keta—
it might not long remain.

THEY'RE TEARING
UP THE OLD GRAVEYARD

They're tearing up the old graveyard
Behind the boarding school;
Bulldozers scrape off the headstones
And grind them in the mud.

That way there will remain no names
To link with battered bones;
That way there will be left no spot
To bring back memories.

Oh we may not have known by face
The skulls they soon will desecrate.
But the names—how we still cherish
Each single one as part of us.

We lay on these memorial mounds
And memorised Macbeth and maths;
We climbed these pear and pawpaw trees—
We ate their fruits, dreamt in their boughs.

They say some man, recently rich,
Must have a mansion made
And chose this lovely spot on which
To vent his vanity.

No one who could cared to say no.
And we—what right have we?
They're tearing up the old graveyard
They're tearing down our past.

Kofi Anyidoho

(b. 1947)

Born in Wheta in coastal Ghana, Anyidoho earned his first degree from the University of Ghana, Legon. He also holds an M.A. in folklore from Indiana University, Bloomington, and a Ph.D. in comparative literature from the University of Texas, Austin. He has taught at Cornell and Northwestern Universities, and is currently teaching at the University of Ghana, Legon. His poetry publications are Elegy for the Revolution *(1975),* A Harvest of Our Dreams *(1984),* Earthchild with Brain Surgery *(1985), and* AncestralLogic & CaribbeanBlues *(1995). He is coeditor of the 1988 BBC prize-winning anthology,* The Fate of Vultures. *He has won many poetry awards, including the BBC Arts and Africa Poetry Award (1981), the Davidson Nicol Prize for Verse, and the Langston Hughes Prize in Ghana. A leading figure of the new poetry in Africa, Anyidoho's poetry is highly indebted to his Ewe culture, especially in the use of folklore and oral poetic devices.*

THEY HUNT THE NIGHT

They sought to put us away like
memories of a bad marriage of youth
But like wounds from naughty childhood days
We leave a perpetual scar upon
the forehead of their joy.

We are the dog who caught the game
but later sat beneath the table
over bones over droppings from the mouth.
In gentle tones the master talks of angels
coming down with gifts for God's children
Still we sing of ghosts who would not go to hell.
They hunt the night from cottage door to palace gate
knocking with boney skinny hands, scaring away
God's own children from playing fields at heavensgate.

So they seek to muzzle our howls, to chain our anguish
to their gates of hell. Maybe tomorrow they will
sweep us all into garbage cans with other testimonials
of their greed. But on wings of flames we'll rise and
float across their joys and rain rumours of blood
upon their festive dreams: Rumours Dreams Blood.

(Bloomington, 15 October 1978)

ELEGY FOR THE REVOLUTION

a feverish psyche gropes for an
eye in the shrines of Xebieso
the armoured hope lies exposed
to wrath of thunderbolts

    These feet have kissed the sands of many shores
    Today they lay in cramps, crushed by revolving wheels of state
    This heart has felt the warmth of love, throbbed to
    beats of a thousand joys let loose upon a festive world
    Today it is a husk of corn blown before the burning grass

The Revolution violates a devotee. Beware
Beware the wrath of thunderbolts
The agonised thoughts of a detainee translate
our new blunders into nightmares of blood & sweat:
    whips slashing through tender skins, broken bones
    collapsing to floors of cells, tortured moans
    bursting through concrete walls
    tearing through clouds and skies
    They seek refuge in a house of storms
    and a sad conscience clears a path
    for poison arrows of gods of wrath

From sheltered yards of our righteousness
we watched the loading of an atom bomb
with a doubt on our lips, our cheeks
still blown with mirth of nights of revelry
our drunken ease forgetful of speed of light and sound:
    The muzzled heat of Hiroshima bursts into
    sudden flames, burns our laughter into
    screams. Our crippled mirth wades through
    streams of blood, groping for memories of
    feasts flowing down turbulent gulfs
    half–filled with discarded blue–prints for
    a revolution gone astray into
    arms of dream merchants.

                                         (Legon, 28 February 1976)

TSITSA

And then of course we argued about teachers
those teachers in the school. We all agreed
they really could be funny. I mean sometimes.
There was the big man Masita Matiasi himself.
They say he went to koledzi somewhere up
in the mountains of Amedzofe. Then he went again
to another koledzi also up in the chain
mountains of old Akropong or was it Abetifi?
Now I cannot even tell. Anyway, it was always
on mountains. So when he came down
to this village in the valley his head was full of skies.
He talked about Mawu Yehowa without swallowing saliva.
Maybe Mawu was his Grand Father.
As for Inglishi, he could speak it better than an Ako.
Sometimes his pupils licked those big big words
rolling down his tongue into his he–goat beard.
Sometimes too those rolling words fell down on his belly.
He had the belly of a toad and he always
talked pulling up his ancient trozasi.

MURMURING

I met a tall broadchest
strolling down deepnight
with my fiancée in his arms
She passed me off for a third cousin
on her mama's side of a dried–up family tree

I nodded and walked away
murmuring unnameable things to myself

(Legon, 10 May 1978)

OUR BIRTH-CORD

> a piece of meat lost in cabbage stew
> it will be found   it will be found

If we must die at birth, pray
we return with our birth-cord still uncut
our oneness with Earth undefiled

Last night on the village square a man
bumped into my conscience and cursed
our god. I refused to retort, knowing
how hard it is for man to wake a man
from false slumber
Our conscience would not be hurt
by threats of lunatics

> a pinch of salt lost in cabbage stew
> it will be found   the tongue will feel it out

We heard their cries but thought of dogs
and ghosts. Ghosts gone mad at dogs
who would not give our village a chance
to sleep, to dream
Now they say we have to die
These brand-new men gone slightly drunk
on public wine they say we have to die

Yet if we must die at birth, pray
we return with our birth–cord still uncut
our name still to be found in the book of souls
Across the memory of a thousand agonies
our death shall gallop into the conference hall of a million hopes
a lone delegate at reshuffling of destinies

> a piece of hope lost in public tears
> it will be found   it will be found

And if we must die at birth, pray
we return with—
But we were not born to be killed
by threats of lunatics
The maimed panther is no playmate for antelopes

Abena Busia

(b. 1953)

Born in Accra, Busia spent her childhood in Holland and Mexico before living in Oxford, England, where she received a B.A. in English and litera-ture, and a Ph.D. in social anthropology. In addition to having been a post-doctoral fellow at both Bryn Mawr College and the University of California, Los Angeles, Busia has taught at Ruskin College, Oxford, and Yale University. She currently teaches at Rutgers University. She has pub-lished a collection of poems titled Testimonies of Exile (1994). In her poet-ry there is tension between exile and home, contrasting influences that are played out in her consciousness.

EXILES

Funerals are important,
away from home we cannot lay
our dead to rest,
for we alone have given them
    no fitting burial.

Self conscious of our absence,
brooding over distances in western lands
we must rehearse,
the planned performance of our rites
    till we return.

And meanwhile through the years,
our unburied dead eat with us,
follow behind through bedroom doors.

ILLICIT PASSION

All our dreams are possible,
that is the danger:

the desert yields
to an impossible bloom:
a devouring magical beauty
straining for rain through a scarred earth
hiding traces of abandoned lives.

MAWU OF THE WATERS

I am Mawu of the Waters.
With mountains as my footstool
and stars in my curls
I reach down to reap the waters with my fingers
and look, I cup lakes in my palms.
I fling oceans around me like a shawl
and am transformed
into a waterfall.
Springs flow through me
and spill rivers at my feet
as fresh streams surge
to make seas.

Naana Banyiwa Horne

(b. 1949)

Born in Kumasi, Horne's family moved to Accra when she was four years old. She was educated both in her native Ghana and in the United States, where she received an M.A. and a Ph.D. in English. After working in Florida, she currently teaches at Indiana University, Kokomo. She has published her poetry in Asili: Journal of Multicultural Heartspeaks *and* Obsidian II. *Her poetry, while being pro-women, questions Western feminism, and shows her good sense of humor and sarcasm.*

MESSAGES

anyemiyoo
do you remember *oshimashi?*
In our heyday
the prospect of spending
even a little time with him
we considered so preposterous
the thought of it would send us
giggling
and then we would fittingly
punctuate our contempt with
a hiss
hissing
as only highly affronted ghanaian females
could hiss

rokpokpo
that was our nickname for him
remember?

rokpokpo
a name inspired by the mere look
of his clothes which were in cahoots
with some invisible force to obey the wind

of course
knowledge of the man inside the clothes
made evident we could not have chosen
a more fitting name for him
he definitely was as flaky as his *rokpokpo* clothes

ei *anyemiyoo*
now I hear
oshimashi with his *rokpokpo* self is an officer of state
the wind has blown him right into the lap of opportunity

his *rokpokpo* clothes are now
gone with the wind
he sports three piece suits custom–made in
paris and rome

his ashen blotchy skin has followed suit
he looks like a candidate
for a skin tone cream commercial
when he is not jetsetting and hobnobbing
with our former slavers
he is lulling around
in a plushly carpeted airconditioned office
in that castle by the sea

anyemiyoo
I hear *oshimashi rokpokpo*
has sworn vengeance
on all those who did not see his worth
when it was shrouded in *rokpokpo* clothes

he sent a friend to warn us
he wants us to know it is not too late for us
to make his special guests list

of course
you know how I answered his messenger
first I giggled
just like the old days
and then
I hissed
I hissed long and sensuous
I hissed
as only a mature ghanaian woman
who doesn't give a damn about the
rokpokpos of the world can
hiss

A NOTE TO MY
LIBERAL FEMINIST SISTER (1)

the issue for me
sister
is not whether I have been
knocked up or knocked down
borne unwanted children from sexual
acts to which I did not give my consent
it is not to count how many times
a fist has been slammed into my jaw
an unwanted penis thrust into my vagina
befouling eyes devoured my body on the job
while I desperately strive to convince I am
the brain for which I was hired to do the job
sister
I cannot wallow in self pity or internalize victim status
neither do I have the luxury to immortalize
my victimization by making art of my degradation
playing victim scenes over and over
like a broken needle caught
in the same groove on the record
unable to play the entire song out
really, sister
do we have time to quibble about whether
I am in denial, repressed, or simply so
frequently abused that I have lost
consciousness of what constitutes abuse?

The real question for me
sister
is how I am going to rise from the ground up
after I have been knocked down
keep a song in the hearts of all my children
wanted and unwanted
it is how we are going to manage to stay up
and avoid being dragged back down
that struggle, sister
is enough to consume whatever energies
we have left considering all the ways
invented to keep us down on the ground

Kojo Laing

(b. 1946)

Born in Kumasi, Laing was educated in Ghana and then Scotland, where he obtained an M.A. Once secretary of the Institute of African Studies at the University of Ghana, Legon, he has for many years been running St. Anthony's, a private school founded by his mother. In addition to his poetry collection, Godhorse *(1994), he has published two novels,* Search Sweet Country *and* Woman of the Aeroplanes. *His poetry is unorthodox and often displays a shocking and humorous exploitation of traditional subjects and themes.*

STEPS

The big man in batakari
with roses in his mouth
            feels
he is so important
that one step for him
            is
a hundred for others,
            one smile
a thousand laughs,
            one death
a million slaughters.
Really big:
and one itch countless
            scratches.

I AM THE FRESHLY DEAD HUSBAND

I am the freshly dead husband,
I write my death to a fashionable wife:
Dear Dede with the new-bought guarantees, Dede
with the obsession to push hurriedly some
shared memories into my crowded box, crowded
with the two parts of me that were still alive:
   brain and popylonkwe
      still vibrant above the desolation of my other parts,
         above the rotting of my stylish wrists.
I was not properly dead,
I could hear you chat prettily as I lay in state . . .
       and what a state, involving an accident
         with a supertobolo girlfriend still alive . . .
With a funeral cloth of the best style, paid
from the breathless anticipation of my retiring benefits.
Boxes and benefits, hearts and betrayal, ginnnnn!
       How can you mourn me!
To shed tears you had to borrow
from the sorrow of your father's funeral
held last year, when I couldn't cry.
Together my actions and your inventions pushed
all grief to the children who,
not knowing any better, loved my carefree syncopations.
Dede with the black–brown eyes
       whose shades were deeper in the left eye, I
salute your show of courageous grief when
you convinced my mother of the authenticity of your tears!
Bless you, your grief was becoming so successful
that you were, with decorum, fantastically enjoying my death.
I am dead but hungry for guavas . . .
I foolishly imagined the rainbow,
               with its inappropriate joy,
torn from a sky that never gave me any sign till I was dead.
Dede, don't let them push my hearse so fast, have
a little posthumous consideration
         for my erection of the after–life:
a dead man can't go to God with his popylonkwe at attention.

God forgive your speed
for you want to disgrace me before the ancestors!
Hurrying to bury me . . .
hey wait, the erection still stands . . .
was the horror for my mother, whose
tears, so bewildered, could not quite reach me
                        in my wooden flagless castle . . . she
was beginning to sense a picnic atmosphere,
demure girls danced in their walk by my grey skin
                now spiritual at last, at last.
                And I wish my funeral would panic!
Dede I agree I often betrayed you, usually
just at the point when you were
                        simultaneously betraying me, I
imprisoned you in my successes and excesses,
I took your gin and doubled it.
As I speak these words,
fresh ants crawl over me with their white eggs, I
noiselessly knock and bite my coffin! For
it is too tight for me to wear, I need a different size!
Dede, help me, I demand air-conditioning, I need
the coolness now that you never gave me! But
your back is turned, you adjust your duku in the mirror.
You look in great fashion by my rotting chin.
Did you really have to try so hard
to stop yourself from laughing, as
you realised that I was dreaming
about being buried next to that girl that I REALLY loved!??
And she did burst out laughing as the last dust covered me . . .
And her laughter said: I was truthful about all my boxed lies.
Yes, but I will write again!
I see the ginnnnn of resurrection glass to glass!

Kwadwo Opoku–Agyemang

(b. 1951?)

Born and educated in Ghana, Opoku-Agyemang was a Fulbright scholar at Clark University, Atlanta, from 1988–1990. He currently teaches at the University of Cape Coast in Ghana. His two collections of poetry are Cape Coast Castle *(1995) and* Seoul Eyes *(1997). In both collections, he writes about simple experiences that lead to deep contemplation.*

KING TUT IN AMERICA

To Cheikh Anta Diop

THEY MADE the good king pass
They bleached his skin
Cooked his hair
and turned his lips
But after 3000 years
who could turn his head?

In the night when no one was looking
they turned off the lights
Lifted his face
Fixed his nose
Cut his name in pieces
And sealed his lips
They then charged the experts
To invent a new source for the Nile
Still they could not turn his head

I swear, I too saw King Tut
And even in profile
and beneath all that make–up
he was still smiling
After 3000 years he has not paled
So why should we?

Ahmed Tidjani–Cisse

(b. 1947)

⌐

Born in Conakry, Tidjani-Cisse left Guinea as a teenager for France, where he studied law and political science. He currently teaches African dance and directs an African ballet troupe in Paris. He has published a collection of poems, Pollens et Fleurs *(1980), and a play. His poetry, as in "Home News," deals with the native coping in an exile or foreign situation, a growing dilemma for many African writers abroad; and which dramatizes the postcolonial condition in which they find themselves. The following poem was translated from the French by Gerald Moore.*

HOME NEWS

"My dear son I am well thanks be to God
I pray for you day and night."

"My dear brother it's my sad duty to announce
the death of our beloved mother
which occurred last Sunday
after a short illness."

"My cousin I've grown a lot
send me some trousers and new shoes."

"My love, it's now ten years I've been waiting for you
what's keeping you there in the white man's land
think of the trouble you cause us
by such a long absence."

"My dear friend our country's changing
into a huge shanty-town.
No one can eat his fill except . . .
Send me a tape-recorder."

"My dear son it is I your father
I beg you to return to your land
if not you will not have even
the sorrow of recognizing my tomb."

"My dear nephew, I must tell you
of your father's death
we all hope you'll be able to attend
the forty-days' wake."

"My dear . . ."
A tear yesterday when the postman passed
Anxiety today in waiting for his return
The abyss of sadness envelopes me
When I have no news from home
My soul shrivels a little
When home news tumbles over me.
The other day I made a fleeting boat
Full of home news.
I set it in the water at the wharf of Exile-Overseas.
I went to attend its arrival
at the landing stage of Loneliness-under-Hope.
My boat landed some secret passengers for me
Next day the postman's prophetic hand was
stretched towards me.

"My dear friend, your mother was arrested
last week in reprisal
for your political work against the government
Your family is left without a head
Send me a shirt and a neck-tie."

Oumarou Watta

(b. 1951)

Born in Gaya, Watta attended the Lycee Nationale in Niamey and the Ecole Normale at Zinder, where he received a teaching diploma. He received a B.A. from the University of Niamey. After studying in Colchester, England, he went to the State University of New York at Albany, where he obtained his Ph.D. After teaching at the University of Niamey, Watta moved to the United States, where he currently teaches at the University of New Orleans. He has published a collection of poems, In-Sign-E, which blends the traditional proverbs and thought patterns of the Hausa and Zarma-Songhay languages of Niger with his own knowledge of English.

A STONE AT THE TIP OF THE TONGUE

A dena ga tin

That which the mouth cannot utter
Lies at the tip of the tongue
There it bears a stone
That holds
All that is
Without a name
I wonder
why tempestuous whirlwinds do not pull out
Of this black mass
Or have they forgotten their rage?
Or is rage rooted in the tip of the tongue?

CLOUD RAINS

—*Tashin hankali, gobaran geme*
—*Da sabbi'ze bon gobara, ifo n'i ga wi da?*
(*Buru hari*)

Palm–trees do have
A certain charm
When their woven leaves
Are on fire
Only cloud rains can
Put it out
what shakes the mind
Of the sage
Is the burning of his beard
He does not wait for the cloud rains

Catherine Acholonu

(b. 1951)

Born in Imo State, Nigeria, Acholonu was educated in Nigeria and Germany, where she obtained an M.A. and a Ph.D. While teaching at Alvan Ikoku College of Education, Owerri, she published two collections of poetry, The Spring's Last Drop (1985) and Nigeria in the Year 1999 (1985). In recent years, she has been involved in practical politics in Nigeria. In her poetry, she shows approval for traditional African values and practices as they pertain to women, especially in upholding the roles of wife and mother.

THE WAY

this
     is the way
that
     is the tree

I can climb the *akwu* and
pluck the silk cotton seeds
but these beads of coral
drag me down

take off this regalia
these ivory anklets
cripple me with weight

I cannot save
     the drowning child
cut off these ropes
and set me free
I want to paddle
my astral canoe.

THE SPRING'S LAST DROP

I can still recall their laughter
as they spoke of "lost virtue."
I, Obianuju
I have learned to live in scarcity.

So, cautiously,
I choose my steps
labouring up the steep hill
bearing on my head
in a clay pot
the spring's last drop

but from the bushes
a sweet melody
streams forth
and fills my ears
disarming
tantalising

and the body
is tempted to sway
leading the feet
off the straight path

and the eyes
are tempted to stray
to find the source
the giver of temporal joy

but I must hold fast
my pot of spring water

though the seller of clay pot
      never makes the "customer"
though the carrier of the clay pot
      be the mother of an only son
and though this tune
      vibrating in my ears
      tempts me to dance
      to sway my hips
      in unison
      with it
      beguiling

yet I cannot lose it

      this stem
      this prop

      I have laboured up this hill
      through toil and sweat
      and I cannot spill it

      this water so pure
      so clear so sweet
      the dying spring's last drop

I Obianuju
I shall provide my children
with plenty
I shall multiply this drop
      shall multiply this drop
      shall multi . . . pl . . . p . . .

HARVEST OF WAR

something is taking its course
    wailing echoes
    and re–echoes
    through long corridors
    of life and death
    where four roads meet
    where two roads cross
    where four roads meet
    there is coming
    and there is going

    allow me to use
    your oval passage
    o maid
    after the hospitality
    after a sojourn
    of nine moons

    may I wriggle
    through
    the bush–path

    there are streams
    of blood yet to be spilt

I crossed the seven seas
and planted myself
a seed that grew
in water and blood

and now
to let me a lease of life
she lies
plucking pangs of pain
gliding on the chess–board
of life and death

forgotten is the ecstasy
the pineapple–sweet apple
mutually devoured

it's harvest time
the farm is all ablaze
and she
undaunted and fearless
searches the heart of the fire
for the seed
that planted itself
in water
and blood

it knows neither day nor night
neither war nor peace
no danger even in the face of death
a world in a world
a subtle settler

another harvest
and you wet the soil
with teardrops
bring a spade
bring a coffin

      there are no more coffins
      wrap it up wrap it up in a mat

Funso Aiyejina

(b. 1950)

Born in Edo State, Aiyejina was educated at the Universities of Ibadan, Acadia (Canada), and the West Indies. He taught for many years at the University of Ife before leaving to teach in the West Indies—where his wife is from. He was a visiting Fulbright scholar in the United States during the 1995/96 academic year. In addition to being featured in journals and anthologies, Aiyejina has published a collection of poems, Letters to Lynda & Other Poems *(1990). His poetry is suffused with traditional African oratory.*

MAY OURS NOT BE

May ours not be like the story
of the Ear and the Mosquito;
but if it is, remember, o plunderers,
the Mosquito's eternal vow of protest,
for we shall become like lice
forever in your seams,
ant–heads that even in death
burrow deep into the flesh,
chameleon faeces that cannot
be wiped off the feet,
and regenerating earthworms
that multiply by their pieces;
if there is no rainbow in the sky,
we know how to create one
by splashing water in the face of the sun;
if sleepers' hands protect their ears,
mosquitoes must learn to bite at their legs
to awaken them into their broken pledges;
if treasure hunters disturb our Orukwu rockhill,
thunders will break behind our tongues of lightning
like arrows in flight . . .

WHEN THE MONUMENTS . . .

For Walter Rodney and Ngugi wa Thiong'o

When the monuments to our past
are whittled down by new facts
and our dew drops of change
are sacrificed on the altar of state security,
we awake to the knowledge that
pebbles lodged in muddy ponds
must grow muddy with time . . .

Now that our messiahs have chased our dreams
from the sacred corners of our hearts
into the blind alleys of our ghettoes
where they proceed to slaughter them
before our astonished imagination
summoning history to witness their feast,
it is time we rejected those who
have severed the link between prayer and miracles,
those who mock our voices with giant signboards
which proclaim only fairy-tale projects
and those who make us build the podia
on which they stand to salute our misery
on every anniversary of the revolution.

THE DIALOGUE

Perched on his balcony of pleasure,
beside a range of gifts,
the King asked the Poet
who stood below to pay homage:
"How are my people faring
on this beautiful day?"

The Poet stretched his ostrich neck
and readied the traditional trick
of "We thank our God and our King by whose twin grace
our heads still sit on our necks . . ."
but the lie choked his weaverbird throat,
and instead he answered:
"Your Highness, your people are too hungry
to see the beauty of any day;
things are getting worse by the day
as we wait for the better days
which you promised this time last season,
the same promise we've always heard
from the echo of every voice
that has ever occupied that throne
upon which you sit."
Livid, like a seven–barrelled thunder
the King withdrew with his gifts
and the Poet starved with the people.

Ifi Amadiume

(b. 1947?)

*Educated in Nigeria and then in Britain, where she completed her doctor-
ate program at the University of London, Amadiume combines creative and
scholarly interests. After working in England for some years, she currently
teaches at Dartmouth College in the United States. She has published two
collections of poetry,* Passion Waves *(1986), a runner-up for the
Commonwealth Poetry Prize in 1986, and* Ecstasy *(1993). She has also
published* Male Daughters, Female Husbands *(1987), on Igbo culture. Her
poetry is simple, candid in private themes, and exhorts women to be sincere
and free in self-expression.*

BITTER

If you were to squeeze me and wash,
squeeze me and wash,
squeeze me and wash,
and I foam,
again and again,
like bitter–leaf
left out too long to wither,
you would not squeeze
the bitterness out of me.

OYA NOW

By the time they are finished
with filing and colouring their nails,
where is the time?
where is the time?

By the time they are finished
with straightening and curling their hair,
where is the time?
where is the time?

By the time they are finished
with lightening and pampering their skins,
where is the time?
where is the time?

Where is the will
to suck in your breath
pull up
and tighten your *wrappa*
hold it well well with your *oja*
and say *oya*!
wata don pass *gari*—o!
once and for all—o!
make we settle this thing—o!
now now!
oya—o!
oya!
oya o!
oya now!

4TH WITNESS—THE PETTY THIEVES

The eye sees, but not itself!
The rat says it steals,
because nobody has given it its own share!
We have nothing to lose now,
for flaying cannot hurt a goat
that has already been slaughtered!

Ezenwa–Ohaeto

(b. 1959)

Educated at the Universities of Nsukka and Benin, Ezenwa-Ohaeto taught at the Advanced Teachers College of Ahmadu Bello University and the Anambra College of Education, Awka, before leaving for Alvan Ikoku College of Education at Owerri, Imo State. He has also been a resident scholar in Mainz, Germany. His poetry publications include Songs of a Traveller *(1986),* I Wan Bi President *(1988), and* Voice of the Night Masquerade *(1986). He has won many prizes, including the BBC Arts and Africa Poetry Award (1981), best free verse poem in* Orphic Lute *(1985), and the Association of Nigerian Authors/Cadbury Poetry Award (1997). In addition to publishing a biography of Chinua Achebe, Ezenwa-Ohaeto has also written a book of essays on Nigerian literature. His poems in pidgin English have reinvigorated the poetic art as a popular medium of his generation.*

I WAN BI PRESIDENT

E get one dream
wey dey worry me
I don dream am tire,

If I sleep small
Na di dream go come
If I close eye small
Na di dream go come
If I siddon for chair
say make I rest small
Na di dream go come
I think say na malaria dey come,

For night when I lie for bed
When hunger dey blow me
When I never see food chop
When I never see water drink
Na di dream go come,

E get one dream
wey dey worry me
Di dream bi say
I wan bi President,

I never see President hungry
I never see President thirsty
President no go worry for road
Police no go stop am for checking
President no go worry for house
Na government cook dey make food
Na government driver dey drive motor
Na him make I wan bi President,
President de go where e like
President dey do wetin e like
If President wan travel
Na siren dey clear road
param param piroo piroo
Every car go run comot for road too
Na President dey pass for road,

Dem go close di road
Dem go close even air too
Dem go take one car carry am
Dem go take another one dey follow
All dem vehicle tyre dey new
All dem vehicle engine dey new
Di seat go clean well well
Na President get country

I never see President walk ten mile
If e wan go give person message,
I never see President begin cry
If e no se motor wey go carry-am
I never see President push truck
From morning reach night
Even if e no find ten kobo chop,

I never see President go farm
With hoe wey don spoil finish
De day e dey plant crop for farm
Na him make I wan be President,

If you see President him servant
Dem body dey fat well well
If you see President him wife
She go dey smile as e dey happy
If you see President him children
Na guard go dey follow dem
Na special treatment dem go get
Na'im make I wan bi President,
President dey different different sha!
Some President dem dey
Wey no dey win election
Some President dem dey
Wey no dey lose election
Some President dem dey
Wey dey rule forever,

President dey different different
Some President dem dey
Wey dey make ideology
Dey look like person wey no see food chop
Some President dem dey
Wey dey worry make dem country better
You go see suffer for dem face
Some President dem dey
Wey dey kill person like dem bi flies
If you frown face na firing squad
If you say you no see food chop
Na bullet you go see chop one time
Some President dem dey
Wey don fat like person we dey for fattening room
President dey different different

If President go oversea
Na for red carpet e go walk
Na so so salute dem go dey make
na special aeroplane go carry am
Na for best hotel e go sleep
Dem fit give am special woman sef for night
President fit take cocaine travel too
E fit carry heroin dey go
e fit bring hemp return
Dem no dey search President,
I wan be President like Russia dem own
If him sneeze every country go begin cry
I wan be President like America dem own
If him cough every country go begin weep,

I wan be President
If I wan marry beautiful wife
I go order make she come
If I wan chop better food
I go order make dem go bring am
If I wan girlfriend sef
Na so I go send driver for evening,

I wan bi President
for work no go dey trouble me
I go dey make enjoyment as I like
Person go write my speech
Person go drive di car
I fit send person sef make e go read am,

I wan bi President
If food no dey market I no worry
If dem say price don rise I no go worry
If salary no come on time I no go worry
If petrol dey cost too much I no go worry
If sanitation exercise dey I no go worry
If na religion trouble dey I no go worry

I wan bi President
make people enjoy too
     Wetin bi federal character
Every industry go dey there
     Wetin bi disadvantaged area
Every appointment go go there
     Wetin bi geographical spread
every promotion go bi for dem
Federal character na for person wey no get broda,

I wan bi President
We dem go dey praise
Every street go carry my name
I go rename all university for di country
All di town go carry my name
If dem publish newspaper or magazine
Wey curse me even small
Na bomb I go take teach dem lesson

If I dey pass for road
Every person go stand dey wave

I wan bi President
Make I get plenty titles
Dem go call me de Excellency
I go bi Commander–in–Chief
I fit bi Field Marshall and Admiral
I go bi Lion of de Niger
I go answer Grand Commander of di Nation
Dem go address me as snake wey get forest,

My broda
I wan bi President
Even for my Papa House

But na dream I dey dream.

Angela Miri

(b. 1959)

Born in Plateau State, Miri studied at the Universities of Maiduguri and Jos, where she obtained an M.A. and a Ph.D. Her doctoral dissertation was on the oral literature of her Mernyang people. She currently teaches at the University of Jos. In her poetry, she expresses a determination to be freed from limitations placed on women by African patriarchies.

DO NOT STOP ME!

Do not stop me!
I burn
like the wild harmattan fire,
burning uncontrollably
and destroying everything in its path
to clear the sloth for a carnival!
No amount of water or jet of liquid chemicals
can quench this thirst
in me for self-expression.

Full to the brim,
I overflow
and someone there unimpressed
and beguiled of words
potent enough to smash his spine.

I regale in divine endowments
to fire on, exploring until doomsday.
Do not stop me now,
there is no room
to contain me,
I have let loose in the firmament.
Yet I must give control
and save what is left of my being
lest I empty all and lose all!
But do not stop me!

Chimalum Nwankwo

(b. 1945)

Born in eastern Nigeria, Nwankwo began his secondary education in Zaria and Okigwe before earning a B.A. from the University of Nigeria, Nskukka. He later obtained M.F.A., M.A., and Ph.D. degrees from the University of Texas, Austin. After teaching in Nsukka and at East Carolina University, Greenville, he currently teaches at North Carolina State University, Raleigh. He has published three collections of poetry, Feet of the Limping Dancers, Toward the Aerial Zone, *and* Voices from Deep Water. *He was the joint winner of the Association of Nigerian Authors' Poetry Prize in 1988. There is a sarcastic and humorous edge to much of his poetry. In addition, there is great indebtedness to Igbo oratorical devices.*

POEM

in sand
all the ostriches
had their heads

in their heads
all the ostriches
had sand

ASPHALT

For D. I. Nwoga

Night darkens the middle of the road
Like stone night has dropped over our mid-work

Ibeakwadalam Nwoga!
You were with us
At the edge of our great forest
At mid–morning

Ibeakwadalam Nwoga!
You were with us
At the felling of the trees
For black asphalt

Ibeakwadalam Nwoga!
When the festival drum rolled
You were with us
To cup sweat in gourds of mirth

Alas! The big drum has called
Death has called across the seven rivers
And you have answered like a stalwart

Night darkens the middle of the road
Night like stone has dropped over our mid-work

Ibeakwadalam Nwoga!
When words became steel blades
You stood like a sacred iroko
And stared the blades blunt

When we looked for signs
You saw the crescent moon
And understood
As you saw yam tendrils
And understood—
Our bonfires were from what
You understood—
You knew the drizzle
That will bear a storm
And read the harvest news
On the harmattan's face

Ibeakwadalam Nwoga!
Once I heard you sing of twilight
At noontide
And when you called a snake a rope
We understood
Master of the language of deep nights
We understood

Night darkens the middle of the road
Like stone night has dropped over our mid-work

Ibeakwadalam Nwoga!
Your eyes were seven through bramble and vine
Black asphalt grows
Asphalt grows with our ancestral paths
Black asphalt grows
Who will mark with us the ancestral heels
Black asphalt grows
Who will mark where the next trees fall
Who will tell the trees to be pruned?

Night darkens the middle of the road
Like stone night has dropped over our mid-work

Ibeakwadalam Nwoga!
We will remember you when we need fire
When tinders burn for new asphalt
And bush smoke rises into the sky
We will remember you
No power can eat Death
Not even the arrogant sun
But Death cannot eat memories
We will remember you when we need light—

When palm fronds and sacred ferns mark differences
And need wisdom as cutlasses
When fire coals drop from the mouth of bards
From the ancient homesteads at Aguleri
And need goatskin bags that will not burn
When the great hills at Nsukka
Turn into spirits and spirits into hills
And we need seven eyes
When stalwarts ride their hot blood
And answers wait in an elder's hut

When broken women brim with tears
And look for peace on soft shoulders
When children quiz their parents' faces
For the warmest voice from the last festival—
Where is Ijele, great mask of many mirrors
Where is Ijele, resplendent in a thousand colours?

We will remember your voice
At the crisis-point of our fevers
We will remember your work
Like great medicine from the past

Ibeakwadalam Nwoga!

Odia Ofeimun

(b. 1950)

*Ofeimun studied political science at the University of Ibadan. His first col-
lection,* The Poet Lied, *is generally seen as the beginning of the new poetry
in Nigeria, because of both its artistic qualities and its controversial criti-
cism of a section of the Nigerian literary elite during the country's civil war
from 1967 to 1970. Once a political adviser to Nigerian veteran politician
Chief Obafemi Awolowo, Ofeimun has been working as a print journalist in
Lagos. He has been both secretary and president of the Association of
Nigerian Authors (ANA). His second collection of poems is titled* A Handle
for the Flutist.

PROLOGUE...

I have come down
to tell my story
by the same fireside
around which
my people are gathered

I have come home
to feel for ears and hearts and hands
to rise with me
when I say the words
of my mouth

And I must tell my story
to nudge and awaken them
that sleep
among my people.

THE NEW BROOMS

The streets were clogged with garbage
the rank smell of swollen gutters
claimed the peace of our lives

The streets were blessed with molehills
of unwanted odds and bits

Then, they brought in the bayonets
to define the horizons of our days
to keep the streets clear
they brought in the new brooms

To keep the streets clear
they brought in the world–changers
with corrective swagger–sticks
they brought in the new brooms
to sweep public scores away.

But today listen today
if you ask why the wastebins are empty
why refuse gluts the public places unswept
they will enjoin you to HOLD IT:
to have new brooms, that's something.

And if you want to know why
the streets grunt now
under rank garbage
under the weight of decay, of nightsoil
more than ever before
they will point triumphantly, very triumphantly
at their well–made timetable:

"We shall get there soonest;
nightsoil clearance is next on the list."

SONG

You are the sandstorm beneath my skin
the salt in the raw bleeding flesh

You are the flagellation and the herb

You are the hurricane of my restless nights
the conversation that soon becomes an argument

You are the flagellation and the herb

Into your cup my life runs ever–flowingly
into your agitated arms: my jural mirror

You are the flagellation and the herb

And, when I kneel, it is for you I crave
you are my song: I know no other

Tanure Ojaide

(b. 1948)

Born in Okpara Inland, Delta State, Ojaide was educated in Nigeria and the United States. He has published eight collections of poetry, including Labyrinths of the Delta, The Fate of Vultures, The Blood of Peace, The Endless Song, *and* Daydream of Ants. *He has also published two books of literary essays. A fellow in writing at the University of Iowa and a leading member of the new generation of African poets, Ojaide has won major poetry awards, including the Commonwealth Poetry Prize for the Africa Region (1987), the BBC Arts and Africa Poetry Award (1988), the All-Africa Okigbo Prize for Poetry (1988 and 1997), and the Association of Nigerian Authors' Poetry Prize (1988 and 1994). He taught at the University of Maiduguri in Nigeria before his current appointment at the University of North Carolina, Charlotte. His poetry deals with private and public themes in a simple style that is informed by traditional poetic techniques.*

WHERE EVERYBODY IS KING

Come to Agbarha*
where everybody is king
and nobody bows to the other.
Who cares to acknowledge age, since
power doesn't come from wisdom?
And who brags about youth
when there's no concession to vitality?
You just carry your head high.
And do you ask why
where nobody accepts insults
doesn't grow beyond its petty walls?

---

*There is a traditional Urhobo saying that every indigene of Agbarha is a king.

When you come to Agbarha
mind you, the town of only kings,
there are no blacksmiths, no hunters;
you will not find anybody
doing menial jobs that will
soil the great name of a king—
nobody ever climbs the oil-palm,
nor taps the rubber tree.

Of course, rivalry
has smacked the town
with a bloody face.
No king is safe
or sees himself as really great
in the presence of others.
And they try their diabolic charms
on each other, dying like outcasts
without horn-blasts, without
the communal rituals of mourning.

In Agbarha
nobody wakes to work—
everybody washes his mouth with gin
and sits at home
on a floor-mat of a throne.
Are you surprised
at kwashiorkor princes and princesses,
prostitute queens and beggar kings?
Come to Agbarha
where everybody prides himself greater
than the rest of the world
and see the hole
where kings live their unfortunate lives.

THE FATE OF VULTURES

O Aridon,* bring back my wealth
from rogue-vaults;
legendary witness to comings and goings,
memory god, my mentor,
blaze an ash-trail to the hands
  that buried mountains in their bowels,
  lifted crates of cash into their closets.

I would not follow the hurricane,
nor would I the whirlwind
in their brazen sweep-away;
they leave misery in their wake.
I would not spread my ward's wealth in the open
and stir the assembly to stampede;
I would not smear my staff with the scorn of impotence.

You can tell
when one believes freedom is a windfall
and fans himself with flamboyance.
The chief and his council, a flock of flukes
gambolling in the veins of fortune.
Range chickens, they consume and scatter . . .
They ran for a pocket-lift
in the corridors of power
and shared contracts at cabals—
the record produce and sales
fuelled the adolescent bonfire of fathers.

Shamgari, Shankari, shun *garri*
staple of the people
and toast champagne;
Alexius, architect of wind-razed mansions,
a mountain of capital.
Abuja has had its dreams!

---

*Aridon: god of memory and muse of the Urhobo people of Nigeria.

O Aridon, bring back my wealth
from rogue–vaults;
they had all their free days,
let today be mine.
Cut back pictures of shame
for I know why
        the gasping eagle, shorn of proud feathers
        sand–ridden, mumbles its own dirge
        gazing at the iroko
        it can no longer ascend . . .

Pity the fate of flash millionaires.
If they are not hurled into jail, they live
in the prisonhouses of their crimes and wives
and when they die, of course, only their kind
shower praises on vultures.

A VERDICT OF STONE

You fled this island in a bark,
breaking free from my embrace,
your soul shaped like a prow.
The island shrinks daily, the sea
closer by every step on land.

As I walk down the ruin of old blocks
into homes built on dead bones,
I know you were
Ayayughe of the tales,
gathering firewood after every storm;
pounding yam for the little ones.

No doors open where you weaned
a dozen mouths who swung you here and there;
no windows watch the cherry-tree
(its fruits have lost their savage taste).
There all is abandoned,
except the soil God keeps for His testament.

And here I empty this bottle from my travels
over your head; the ocean deepened our love.
Since you broke faith with flesh,
rags sewn to dress you,
I discern dirt piling and piling up
at the beach, the line between us.

In your flitting twilight, you called
my name with your last breath,
and I held you; but you were already
irrevocably possessed for the endless journey.
Today I call your name, *Amreghe*,
with an elephant tusk;
the island vibrates with your music.

THE DAYDREAM OF ANTS

1

Hunter friend of mine
hide–string this scooped ironwood
through which the wind blows its woes;
hide–string this cylindrical handicraft
into Uhaghwa's music box.

I want to strike hard notes
for the head and hands
that have worked wonders,
and I need to be accompanied
to achieve the voiceful task . . .

2

We are in league with powers
to wreck one vision
with lust for more visions
to refashion a proud world—
with the same hands
that raise a storm of dust,
we paint towers of magnificence.

We bridge craters,
build islands in vast seas;
we have wiped out night
with white fires of fluorescence.
And these are no small wonders,
the handicraft of ants,
a mountain cap over a plain face . . .

3

Man has more than double-built
his manly image of a beast
in the precincts of his daydream.
He has torn apart the human suit
he was born with for good;
now an elephant he charges
and tramples the earth—
everything yields to his boots.
He builds monuments out of mountains.
Seeks bridges across ranges
of abysmal gashes . . .

Must he perform magic
to earn the praisename
of the mammoth of an ant?

WHERE THE NIGHTMARE BEGINS

You are probably dreaming
to go very far in your field,
and you are already living towards it.

When you have gone a long way,
the hopescope will change—
there will be no cowdung to cover you,
no hedges to slip into.
You will then be in the limelight,
the sun–swathed emperor of a vast country.

And there the nightmare begins.
You can always be caught naked
and others will freeze that in their minds—
a photo to brandish before you
when you least need a sore past.

And when you have gone that far,
you become everybody's vision
of a worthy adversary—
you sleep with eyes open
and hands clenched.

You will have to love
the uniform growth
which remained so low
for you to be seen everywhere—
perhaps, an accident; but
don't forget that without feet
firm on the ground,
the head wouldn't be so high.

Upon your arrival,
there's a wholesale offer
of unlimited openness;
and you have to prove others wrong
that you haven't gone this far
only to blow your name into the winds!

Femi Osofisan

(b. 1946)

⌐

Better known for his many plays, Osofisan published his first collection of poems, Minted Coins, *under the name of Okimba Launko. His second collection,* Divining Chains, *was published under his real name. Educated in Nigeria and France, his first collection won the Association of Nigerian Authors' Poetry Prize. He has won many awards in drama, where he is probably the leading dramatist of the new generation. He has brought into his poetry experience of drama, a wealth of folklore, and incantatory rhythm.*

RELEASE

Iwapele, release me
it is time to offer my pollen to the wind

When the once–sacred shrines fill with vulgar masks
& the sibilating chorus of sycophants usurp the air

When Ogun's hammer swings in desecrated hands
& wanton carnage spreads in the forge, to cowed applause

When the acid lips of falsehood lick the newspapers
& amidst the spittle, one swims alone

When the fists of power throttle the daily headlines
& amidst the babble, one strains alone

(& we all have our numerous reasons for silence:
we can stand by a furnace and shun the heat
pleading that we are deaf to the bellows:
we can stand at peace by a grinding saw
with the excuse that it is only morning yet,
that we have not begun to chisel ourselves out
nor shape the contours of our rage . . .)

Release me:
in my belly is the foetus of a struggling scream
I wait, tottering, on the horizon of slogans

Release me, the road is waiting . . .

PARIS LATIN QUARTER

Sweet Marie–Anne, she thought
Being French, intellectual and brunette

Entitled her, in any Parisian cafe
To prompt service—and she was

Probably right, (as the Policeman
Later confirmed)—always provided

The situation was normal, and
She herself did not let the race down.

So that afternoon, she said to me:
"Sit by me, *mon cheri*, and order

A drink!"—Well! The waiter came
As was his duty, only to stand aghast

At the unspeakable scandal of a
Full-blooded French woman kissing

This *merde* of a black man openly and
Full on the lips!—Purebred son of

The Galls, his first impulse
Was to smash his tray at the black head

And shriek out for help to the army of riot
Police permanently stationed on the streets

Of the Latin Quarter . . . —But
He was a non–violent man, and besides,

He had the customer's tip to think of.
So he turned to me, swallowing hard, and

With controlled French politeness, he said:
"*M'sieur*, please sit OPPOSITE the lady—

"Yes, with the *sacre* table between you, face
To face—Or *mon cul*, dammit, I shall
Not serve you!"—And I was still wiping off
Her lipstick, wondering what to do, when my lady

Spoke, her face red with indignation: "But
You're mistaken! This one's not like the rest,

"Can't you see! He's a *bon sauvage*, and has
Written such brilliant essays in impeccable French

"On the phallus of—pardon, the merits of Negritude!
Show him my dear!" she turned to me, "Show how well

"You quote Molière, Corneille, and—"But the waiter
Was already smiling and bowing: I had passed my test.

SHE THINKS IN SONG

For Penima

Oh she thinks in song
because she thinks of us:
my Africa thinks in song—
    Che che kule
    Che Kofi sa . . .

Because she thinks of us
We, for whom tomorrow's household
Is still a rubble of bricks
because our skin was singed
in the kiln of colonial pain:
    Kofisa langa
    Langa ti langa
    Kumba le–le! . . .

Rise, history!—I hear her sing;
she pulls us into the chorus
with her voice, to dance by her side,
the dance which is a promise of a new continent
(& it is not only our hands that are clapping . . .)
    Che che kule . . .

Rise! She says, Africa must come awake!
Rise, because it is not the habit of bricks
to be idle: bricks must grow into homes,
into monuments! . . .
    Kofisa langa . . .

She sings, and—see!—even women from faraway
villages take flesh before us, stand
no longer remote, no longer shadows,
but each like a brown and urgent fist in the air,
smashing into our male complacencies,
shouting for justice, for justice! . . .
      Che Kofi sa
      Kofisa langa
      Langa ti langa . . .

Oh she fights in song,
Woman of the new Africa,
because she fights not alone:
her wrapper is woven of threads
gathered over many seasons of
different griefs and countless lamentations
       Kumba le–le . . .
       Kumba le–le . . .

LISTEN! In her voice, our women
are saying—Africa must be free!
The dirges and the wailings must cease!
Hers is a language of many tongues and many
dialects but a single song!
     Che che kule . . .

Oh woman, woman of such electric tunes
Oh woman of the new Africa
how fluid your body flows like swift currents
along the shores of our green remembering!
How your songs renew the forests of our faith
and prune the rust from our weakening stems!
     Che che kule . . .
     Che Kofi sa . . .

Woman, please continue to dream in song
since you dream us, since you dream of us;
Ablaze, and colourful, at the end of
your waving arms,
the continent again remembers itself
as a strutting flag of freedom
such as we knew, when our youth
was large and unfurling . . .
     Che Kofi sa . . .

Oh your voice is a fire so warm
that many pots shall come to kneel beside it,
bubbling with hope and with spices . . .
Oh woman of Africa, dream
and dream on in song
and we will try to dream along:
for it is not our hands alone that are clapping! . . .

LONGING

Life roars on, of course
elsewhere, as I rise and open the door.

And there is a moon, outside,
shining gently, as if afraid to be heard

It will not tell me of your whereabouts,
the moon does not believe that I miss you

and so, in the fluorescence of my office,
sitting alone with my poem,
I am alone and do not hear you pass

I miss your steps in the corridor of
the century, and the friends are fewer daily
to confide in, except this poem

Except this song that will not be sung.

Niyi Osundare

(b. 1947)

Born in Ikere-Ekiti in Ekiti State, Nigeria, Osundare was educated in Nigeria, Britain, and Canada. Long a professor at the University of Ibadan, he currently teaches at the University of New Orleans in the United States. He is a leading figure of the new African poets and has published seven collections of poems, the best known of which are Songs of the Marketplace, The Eye of the Earth, Moonsongs, *and* Waiting Laughters. *He has won major awards, including the Commonwealth Poetry Prize (1986), the Noma Award for Publishing in Africa (1991), and the Association of Nigerian Authors' Poetry Award (1986 and 1987). Osundare's poetry resonates with oral literary techniques and rhythms. It shows strong concern for the environment and the underprivileged.*

I SING OF CHANGE

Sing on: Somewhere, at some new moon,
We'll learn that sleeping is not death,
Hearing the whole earth change its tune.

W. B. Yeats

I sing
of the beauty of Athens
without its slaves

Of a world free
of kings and queens
and other remnants
of an arbitrary past

Of earth
with no
sharp north
or deep south
without blind curtains
or iron walls

Of the end
of warlords and armouries
and prisons of hate and fear

Of deserts treeing
and fruiting
after the quickening rains

Of the sun
radiating ignorance
and stars informing
nights of unknowing

I sing of a world reshaped.

WHO SAYS THAT DROUGHT WAS HERE

With these green guests around
who says that drought was here?

The rain has robed the earth
in vests of verdure
the rain has robed an earth
licked clean by the fiery tongue of drought

With these green guests around
Who says that drought was here?

Palms have shed the shroud of brown
cast over forest tops
by the careless match of tinder days
when flares flooded the earth
and hovering hawks taloned the tale
to the ears of the deafening sky

With these green guests around
Who says that drought was here?

Aflame with herbal joy
trees slap heaven's face
with the compound pride
of youthful leaves

drapering twigs into groves
once skeletal spires in
the unwinking face of the baking sun

With these green guests around
Who says that drought was here?

And anthills throw open their million gates
and winged termites swarm the warm welcome
of compassionate twilights
and butterflies court the fragrant company
of fledgling flowers
and milling moths paste wet lips
on the translucent ears of listening windows
and the swallow brailles a tune
on the copper face of the gathering lake
and weaverbirds pick up the chorus
in the leafening heights . . .
Soon crispy mushrooms will break
the fast of venturing soles

With these green guests around
who still says that drought was here?

XXII
(from *Moonsongs*)

Ikoyi

> The moon here
> is a laundered lawn
> its grass the softness of infant fluff;
> silence grazes like a joyous lamb,
> doors romp on lazy hinges
> the ceiling is a sky
> weighted down by chandeliers
> of pampered stars

Ajegunle

> here the moon
> is a jungle,
> sad like a forgotten beard
> with tensioned climbers
> and undergrowths of cancerous fury:
> cobras of anger spit in every brook
> and nights are one long prowl
> of swindled leopards

The moon is a mask dancing . . .

XIV
(from *Waiting Laughters*)

Okerebu kerebu
Kerebu kerebu

And the snake says to the toad:
"I have not had a meal
For a good one week;
And my stomach yearns
For your juicy meat"

"Suppose I turn into a mountain?"
Asks the toad

"I will level you in the valley
Of my belly"

"Suppose I turn into a river?"

"You will flow easily through
The channels of my mouth"

"Suppose I become one
Of your favourable children?"

"I will eat you
With all the motherly love
In this world"

The toad then turns into a rock
And the snake swallows it
With delicious despatch

Ah! *Aramonda**
The mouth has swallowed something
Too hard for the mill of the stomach

Okerebu kerebu
kerebu kerebu

Our tale is a bride
Waiting
For the nimble fancy of the grooming ear.

**aramonda:* wonder of wonders!

THE WORD IS AN EGG

My tongue is a pink fire
Don't let it set your ears ablaze

When proverbs clash
In the street of waiting laughters

And murmuring moments eke out
A dirge from the lips of the setting sun

We shall count the teeth
Of the moon

And sing little wreaths
For missing stars . . .

The Word, the Word
Is an egg:

If it falls on the outcrop
Of a stumbling tongue

It breaks
Ungatherably

Mabel Tobrise

(b. 1965)

⸺

Born in Benin City of Delta parents, Tobrise studied theater arts at the University of Ibadan, where she received a B.A., M.A., and Ph.D. Currently teaching at the University of Abuja, she is the editor of Journal of Women in Drama and Society. *Tobrise has been involved in two national arts festivals and the Association of Nigerian Authors. Her manuscript,* Poems Out of Hiding, *deals with themes of womanhood that have not been articulated in Nigerian women's poetry before now.*

DYEING

Weave for me
beautiful patterns
and skeins of silver thread
and gossamer.
I shall sit a while longer
at your loom
while you thread together
the scissored shreds
of this fabric.
Stay at the indigo pit
and with me dip into dye
these tied patterns
of gossamer and silver.
Had I any choice
I would dip them in scarlet,
to mark the end of waiting.

Amadou Lamine Sall

(b. 1951)

Born in Kaolack, Sall attended the University of Dakar. He has published three collections of poetry, Mante des Aurores, Comme un Iceberg en Flammes, *and* Locataire du Neant, *which received honorable mention in the 1990 Noma Award. With Charles Carrere, Sall has coedited a major anthology of African francophone poetry titled* Nouvelle Anthologie de la Poesie Negre et Malgache. *One of the most gifted of the new generation of Senegalese poets, Sall's poetry is intense, simple, and symbolic. The two poems below were translated from the French by Faustine Boateng Gyima.*

LETTER TO A ROVING POET

I don't know where you come from
what name you are so proud of
I don't know from what far away country you are the son
what type of hospitality you have adopted
I don't know whose mother or father
you resemble so much
I don't know what eternal dream you harbour
what solitary hostage you have become
I don't know at what horizon you seem to build your plans
from what love you allow deliverance
I don't know for whom
your heart bubbles with joy
I don't know of what members you are captive
in what jail you live
I don't know what is your fate
what future you are the living dead
I don't know what heaven
which God
I don't know what type of love
you are dove and eagle of fire
all that I must tell you is:
I LOVE YOU

CLOAK OF DAWN

I looked for you everywhere yet nowhere
Between the flower and the stalk
Between day and night
Among laughter of sleep
And the caress of the absent
Where are you daughter of the night
Now the poem is panting and words are scarce
The pen intoxicated with black wine dances
Arabesque vowels are listless
While restive consonants wander in procession
On the empty page that yawns
You will be the only one to understand tonight why
I write this poem . . .
. . . .
Now, when I see you again
You will tell me the time

And later you will tell me the time again
We shall go to buy newspapers of the right and the left
Left–right right–left

I will read them from the east to the west
You will comment on them from north to south
Then we shall disseminate news everywhere
At the four corners of the world of illiteracy and hunger
We shall then go to listen to the politicians
Of all stature and all colours
Very terrible and dangerous liars
. . . .
For it seems that COMMUNISM is to be abolished for peace on
    earth
CAPITALISM to be fought for peace on earth
SOCIALISM to be redefined for peace on earth
But not a single nation has an ideology called
LOVE

We shall live elsewhere
Because God seems to live elsewhere

. . . .
I shall go with you by all available routes
To sow the first seeds of LIBERTY through suffering
We shall build cities without houses or streets
Without prisons or hatred
Where anonymous men without status will come to sleep

. . . .
Manthie I would have loved to lie
To you that no little child is starving in the world
That no mother is crying for a wizened child contorted by a
    bomb
Of a quiet pilot
That no widow is tormented in front of a cadaver
Impossible to express my love

. . . .
To lie to you
That nobody in exile suffers terrible fear
to lie again and again Manthie that

No Apartheid
No Soweto
No Jones-Town
No Red Brigade Army
No Black September
No Lebanon like an immense cake made with blood
No wandering people in Palestine without home
No Israel whose history is persecutor being persecuted,
To lie to you
So that you never recognize their murderous hands

May God transform you into daughter of the night
and that I see tomorrow the candle flame of my people
And of the world
Burning at the altar of great fate
Under the arch of the triple flower of LOVE
of PEACE
of LIBERTY

Syl Cheney-Coker

(b. 1945)

Born in Freetown, Cheney-Coker had his early education there and later attended the Universities of Oregon, California, and Wisconsin, where he studied literature and journalism. After serving as press secretary to Prime Minister Siaka Stevens, he went into voluntary exile and returned to Sierra Leone in 1985 to set up a newspaper. He taught for several years at a university in the Philippines, where he married, and has also taught at the University of Maiduguri, Nigeria. His poetry publications are Concerto for an Exile, The Graveyard Also Has Teeth, *and* The Blood in the Desert's Eye. *He has also published a successful novel titled* The Last Harmattan of Alusine Dunbar. *Cheney-Coker is a very distinguished poet, whose poetry draws upon his Creole ancestry as he deals with private and public themes. His images are strong and his poetry is passionate and well crafted.*

ANALYSIS

I am in my room observing my record player covered with dust
my mountainous library from Brecht to Zola
Pushkin is absent killed in a duel for love
as they die everywhere poets without honour
across the hall Mike snores ferociously
because the landlady let him sleep without his rent
outside the summer smothers the day

the humidity of the summer pissed through the leaves
of every tree. . . . If I dodge the heat tell me which lake
to cool my rage? Lying to your shadow by day the shadow
knows your bright ugliness by night! Ah taste the vinegar
in the air it has more sweetness than my joy

my rage my tears, my groaning, my raving
to whom? For whom? To whom I ask?

to Africa for permitting a perpetual butchery of her womb
to those who barter her on Wall Street and the World Market
muckrakers, smugglers, politicians and the like
to know them by their smiles Wall Street buys your heart!
think of your agony Africa your capitalist war–mongers
those long queues your children straddled strapped to your backs
waiting for those who rule who lead you into the markets of
    slavery
do they sell you for the rand or for the dollar?

to America whose pulse beats too loudly in my heart
your hands your lips your love too vicious to poets
your ladies with false eyelashes who kill your poets
America think of your involvements
those who died with napalm in their eyes
were they necessary for your salvation or for your balance of
    payments?

Cuba is alive in spite of your insane blockade
the Vietnamese shoot through the eyes although you control the
    sky
I am no water fountain the mucus you have poisoned in my
    heart
I die from breathing your air your love is a machine in my heart
but I must think of Africa which is obedient to your dollar

there after you have seen the filth
those who dance under the chandeliers
while others coax the stubborn fires in the huts
you learn that at the price of sanity
you walk with one eye open and the other one shut!

PEASANTS

"The Masters of the Dew"
Jacques Roumain

The agony: I say their agony!

the agony of imagining their squalor but never knowing it
the agony of cramping them in roach infected shacks
the agony of treating them like chattel slaves
the agony of feeding them abstract theories they do not
    understand
the agony of their lugubrious eyes and bartered souls
the agony of giving them party cards but never party support
the agony of marshalling them on election day but never on
    banquet nights
the agony of giving them melliferous words but mildewed bread
the agony of their cooking hearths dampened with unuse
the agony of their naked feet on the hot burning tarmac
the agony of their children with projectile bellies
the agony of long miserable nights
the agony of their thatched houses with too many holes
the agony of erecting hotels but being barred from them
the agony of watching the cavalcade of limousines
the agony of grand state balls for God knows who
the agony of those who study meaningless 'isms in
    incomprehensible languages
the agony of intolerable fees for schools but with no jobs in sight
the agony of it all I say the agony of it all
but above all the damn agony of appealing to their patience
Africa beware! their patience is running out!

POET AMONG THOSE
WHO ARE ALSO POETS

I drive round the dirty streets of Freetown
and observe a man standing at the corner of the library
stabbing his heart with a knife
another spits into the fountain his cola-nut checked hunger
another is crouching half dying under a giant cotton tree
shrieking another with a stream of saliva showering his face
hangs on the gold-plated gates of the presidential palace
and further down a beggar goes by shouting he has been robbed
all in one hour all in one hour

one woman is screaming raped by a bureaucrat
a childless harlot is beaten by another with kids
at the cemetery three women examine their lost treasures in
    bones
three sons like father son and holy ghost
down at the shanty they have turned off the water
because the women have ruined the toilets
and finally a woman has come confessed to selling her daughter

one child whips the other because she called him a dirty name
another is driven to school in a limousine unmarked
while the classmates walk on all ten
at the hospital the wards are in commotion because two children
have been bitten by dogs over at the garbage dump
such is the life seen driving round Freetown.

CHILDHOOD

So late in my life, some things I have remembered:

In the morning I did not wash my face upwards
the trickster had more cards than I dared admit
for him to trick me so, and my childhood uncannily
comes back to me in hiccups

stammering my good morning two words apart
my mother teaches me to speak, watching over
the fall of my stuttered words, the half of my alphabet
swallowed in rage before it was born, being
that I was born the son of my stammering father

my mother trying to loosen my tongue gives me
water out of a bell and the chickens in our yard
scratch, scratch away at my meal to free the grain
of my resolve; my mother speaking on my behalf

and my left–handedness which set my mother thinking:
a cat is a thief, the left-handed child has similar fate
my mother holding my left hand behind my back so that
I will write with my right hand, to be the right son

so late in my life, some things I have remembered:

how they tampered with my brain, the left-sided thought
the right-sided sadness, how endlessly I go the child
of an image in a world that died long, long ago
how my ravaging desert started to spread in my childhood!

DEAD EYES

In the tavern where I slept last night
I went there to forget my bad luck
of a country sinking into neglect

now I am awake, and pulling up my pants
from desire, I say I cannot go back
I have lived so little on remembrance
lived so little on rain, knowing
I have lived so little on my country!

And it is enough that they do not know how it hurts
that in the blue waters of the country they have poisoned
the gentle *dugongs** with the toxic power of their greed
but what can they preserve of that country for me
now that the desire to be man among the scorpions keeps me
    awake
thinking about the tattered history books
the desert which has eaten the heart of the savannah
so that every day Freetown is treacherously poised
above the bay where the capsized canoes
have the hang–dog look of a humanity that has died
Freetown from where they every day sail on their uncertain
    course
as if God had cursed this country shaped like a heart
but without the beauty of a peaceful heart

In the last flicker of your light
let me see the men who are lining
up
to cut up your heart.

---

*dugongs: aquatic mammals with a fish-like body, flipper-like forelimbs, and no
hind limbs; related to the manatee, a seacow.

Iyamide Hazeley

(b. 1957)

Currently based in London, Hazeley spent her formative years in Freetown. She received an M.A. from London University's Institute of Education in 1986. She won a Minority Rights Group/Minority Arts Advisory Service Award for her poetry in 1983 and the Greater London Council Black Experience filmscript competition. She has published a collection of poetry titled Ripples and Jagged Edges *(1987).*

BELOVED

I brought my love
wrapped
in cotton and silk
its face and hands
washed
clean as an innocent.
I cupped my hands
for love to drink from,
filled,
filled
with the sweet
mingling
of joy with fear.
I bared the red,
soft,
centre
where my heart had been
to nourish my beloved
and turn the hunger inside
into a field in harvest.

My love was tumbled to the ground
doused with the salt from my own eyes
then tossed aside in a careless gesture.

He who cannot accept a gift of love
does not deserve it.

LUNGI CROSSING

Early in the morning
after sixteen years away
with still one leg of the journey
remaining,
I arrived home.

The air, the water, the sky
all were tinged
with the blue
of early morning
darkness.

Slowly,
the ferry's motion
through the water
nudged the sun
into the sky.

I leant one foot
and one elbow
against the rails,
watched as children
and grown people
milled about
squeezing past cars
parked cheek by jowl
on the deck.

There we all were.
Those coming
to visit ageing parents
those who came to meet
those coming to visit
those wearing the affluence
of tourists
those bringing home their dead
and those simply
coming home.

WHEN YOU HAVE
EMPTIED OUR CALABASHES

When you have emptied our calabashes
into your porcelain bowls overflowing
the surplus spilling and seeping
into foreign soil
when you have cleaved the heads of our young
and engraved upon the soft papyrus there
an erasure of our past
having built edifices to your lies
filled them with so many bad books and distorts
and sealed the cracks in the structure
with some synthetic daub,
when you stock and pile arms
and talk about the nuclear theatre
want to make the world your stage
limiting the chance of world survival,
it confirms your calculations, your designs
your ambitions which we'll thwart
which we'll resist
which we'll fight in all manner of ways.

We will rebuild
we will choose our most knowing
most eloquent old women
to spit in the mouths
of the newborn babies
so that they will remember
and be eloquent also
and learn well
the lessons of the past
to tell their grandchildren
so that if you come again
in another time
with your trinkets and arms
with porcelain bowls
and scriptures
they will say
we know you.

Notes

1. Ahmed Taha, quoted in Clarissa Burt, "Review Essay: Classical Motifs and Cultural Intertextuality in Contemporary Egyptian Poetry," *Critique* (fall 1995): 106.

2. Clarissa Burt, "The Good, the Bad and the Ugly: The Canonical Sieve and Poems from an Egyptian Avant Garde," *Journal of Arabic Literature* 28 (1997): 147.

3. Clarissa Burt, "Review Essay: Classical Motifs and Cultural Intertextuality in Contemporary Egyptian Poetry," *Critique* (fall 1995): 112.

4. Salma Khadra Jayyusi, ed., *Modern Arabic Poetry—An Anthology* (New York: Columbia University Press, 1987), p. 118.

5. Ibid., p. 224.

Index of Authors

About the Book

This anthology presents the voices of a new generation of African poets, drawn from across the continent and representing a wide range of themes, styles, and ideologies. These contemporary voices have been shaped in the realities of postcolonial Africa from the mid-1970s to the present. In contrast to the preceding generation—forged in the years of nationalist movements and independence—they are less concerned with European culture and colonial oppression and draw more on indigenous poetic and literary techniques than on euromodernist mannerisms.

The poets featured here focus on internal political, economic, and cultural issues in African societies and on their own experiences in the world, revealing a measured self-criticism of the paths their societies are following.

Tanure Ojaide has published eight collections of his own poetry, a memoir, and two books of literary essays, including *Poetic Imagination in Black Africa;* his work has also appeared in numerous anthologies. He is professor of African and African-American Studies at the University of North Carolina, Charlotte. **Tijan M. Sallah,** an economist with the World Bank, is author of three poetry collections, a book of short stories, and an ethnography on Wolof culture; he is also the editor of *New Poets of West Africa* (1995).